100 hikes
IN THE ALPS

IRA SPRING & HARVEY EDWARDS
Photos by Bob & Ira Spring
Maps by Karl Johansen

The Mountaineers • Seattle

The Mountaineers: Organized 1906 " . . . to explore,
study, preserve and enjoy the natural beauty of the Northwest."

Published by
The Mountaineers
715 Pike St., Seattle WA 98101

Published simultaneously in Canada by
Douglas & McIntyre Ltd.
1615 Venables St., Vancouver, B.C. V5L 2H1

Published simultaneously in United Kingdom by
Cordee, 249 Knighton Church Road,
Leicester LE2 3JQ

Manufactured in the United States of America

Edited by Connie Pious
Designed by Marge Mueller

Cover: The Matterhorn and village of Findeln (Hike 28)
Title: Trail to Friesenberghaus and the
    Schlegeisspeicher, Austria (Hike 70)
Photo on page 188 by Harvey Edwards

First edition, first printing June 1979;
second printing May 1982

Library of Congress Cataloging in Publication Data
Spring, Ira.
    100 hikes in the Alps.

    1.   Hiking—Alps—Guide-books.   2.   Alps—Description
and travel—Guide-books.   I.   Edwards, Harvey, joint author.   II.   Title.
GV199.44.A4S68   1979   914.94'7   78-71668
ISBN 0-916890-72-4

INTRODUCTION

Nowhere in the world, in such a concentrated area, can so much varied hiking be found as in the Alps. Hiking in France to the west and in Yugoslavia to the east are vastly different experiences: but only about 1000 km (620 miles) separate these two countries. Between them rise the Alps of Switzerland, Liechtenstein, Germany, Italy, and Austria — countries with their own customs, history, forms of government, distinctive geographic features, and special character. Some are contiguous, but they are very different nevertheless. Proximity, difference, and variety are the words that best sum up hiking in the Alps, as well as the contents of this book.

When I first visited the Alps 30 years ago, I had many questions that are as pertinent today as they were then. Where are the mountain centers? How does one get to the villages, trailheads, passes, summits, lakes, glacier snouts, or castles? What are the trails like? Are they difficult? How long will a hike take—a day, a week, a month? Are the hikes suitable for small children? Can one find camping sites in the valley and above tree level? What are the huts like? Can one pick the flowers and drink the water? At that time, there were no guidebooks to answer such practical, essential questions.

This guidebook has two purposes: to provide basic information on what you will find, and to encourage you to go out and find it. I hope that the photographs, maps, and descriptions will both tempt you and clarify what you are looking for in the mountains. I'm still looking, because for me mountains offer not only the discovery of a very small part of some country, but the discovery of myself as well. Ira Spring, who has been hiking and photographing all over the world for almost 50 years, shares my approach in this guidebook. In our descriptions—researched by Ira, Pat Spring, Vicky Spring, and me—we point out highlights and general landmarks. But we stop there. Our efforts will help you to find the way yourself; we think that through discovery, you will harvest a great deal of personal satisfaction.

With this book and the indicated contour maps, proper backpacking equipment, and common sense, you can explore the Alps from France to Yugoslavia on your own. Professional mountain guides are not necessary in any of these middle-mountain hikes. One other kind of independence deserves mention. We believe that getting up the mountain on your own provides a much richer experience than being whisked to the heights by aerial tram, an airplane equipped for landing on glaciers, or a helicopter. There **are** moments when even we recognize the advantages of mechanical uphill transport, and we note these throughout the book.

Readers may be puzzled by our including five Pyrenees hikes in this book when in fact this mountain range is not, because of its age, part of the Alpine massif. Our justification for including them is that the Pyrenees, which form a natural frontier between France and Spain, provide excellent hiking. We would like backpackers from all over the world to begin to appreciate their special attractions.

Transportation

Through improved train and bus service, as well as the construction of major roads and tunnels, it has become possible to spend an entire summer hiking in all seven of these countries. Up until 10 years ago, most backpackers traveled to and remained at one of the big centers like Chamonix, Innsbruck, or Zermatt. Today, mobility is the key. The Mont Blanc tunnel, connecting France to Italy, and the Italian autostrade (expressways) make it possible to hike the French Alps one day and be in the Dolomites the next. You can catch a fast train from Zurich and be in the Austrian Alps in a few hours. Travel

Chapel at Rifugio Brentei in the Brenta Dolomites (Hike No. 92)

by private automobile can be helpful, particularly if you are camping. You can reach the trailheads easily and have a place to leave your extra gear. On the other hand, European car rentals are expensive, and if you leave a car at a trailhead you must always return to pick it up.

One approach is to try to decide in advance what kind of hiking you want to do and where. For example, it is possible to arrive in Zurich, take a train to Geneva, then a boat to St. Gingolf, and be at the trailhead of the GR 5 (Grande Randonnee or major trail), a 600-km traverse of the French Alps, within a few hours of your arrival in Zurich. Or from Geneva you can go by bus to Chamonix for the start of the three-country Tour du Mont Blanc hike. Or you can fly into Munich, hike around the Bavarian Alps, catch a train to Innsbruck, hike in that area, and continue on to Yugoslavia and Italy—all by train and bus. In Switzerland, trains and busses go where you and the many other hikers want to go.

However, camping can pose problems, particularly in the valleys. It may be far from the railroad station to the campground, or in some small villages there may be no campground at all. This problem is aggravated in Italy, where major cities are often distant from hiking areas. There may be only one train or bus a day going to the mountain village where the trailhead is located. If you miss the bus you can hire a car, hitchhike, walk—or go to the museums in Bolzano or Turin. In any event, don't let one missed bus keep you from hiking in Italy. There are many splendid areas in the Dolomites, along the Italian-French frontier, and in the national parks. Finding the way there is all part of the adventure.

Equipment

Boots are the backpacker's most important piece of equipment. In my opinion, most of the "climbing" boots available on the market are too heavy for middle-mountain hiking. Soles are often extra rigid, making them ideal for climbing but painful and hot on most of the lower trails. Of course, these boots do provide good protection in rain and cold, particularly on the summit of Mont Blanc—or of Mt. Everest, for that matter. But wearing them between 2000 and 3000 meters all day long will make your feet feel like squashed bananas. Unfortunately, I've yet to find in Europe a pair of lightweight, comfortable, flexible, strong, waterproof hiking boots. The best advice is to bring your favorite (and well broken in) hiking boots from home. You can also bring, as I do, a pair of lightweight canvas shoes for the end of the day and easy paved trails.

Wool socks, an extra-large waterproof poncho that can double as a ground cloth, wool gloves, hat, flannel shirt, a pair of shorts, a warm parka, sweater, sunglasses, corduroy or wool knickers, jeans, extra underwear, maps, compass, flashlight with extra batteries and bulb, first aid kit, knife, matches in a waterproof container, some extra food, a paperback or two for the rainy days, and a water bottle—and your pack is pretty much filled. If you are camping, you will want to take along a lightweight tent, sleeping bag and pad, a set of pots, and a small stove. You can get good-quality white gasoline in Europe. In France it's called Essence C and can be purchased in any "droguerie," a store that sells housewares, among other things. To carry it all, I prefer a frame pack, although soft packs are still more popular among the Europeans.

Unless otherwise noted, none of the trails in this book crosses permanent snowfields or glaciers. By mid-July almost all middle-mountain trails are free of snow. However, snow patches may be encountered above 2500 meters in gullies on north-facing slopes. If you want to start hiking before mid-July, or if it has been a year with heavy snowfall, it is sensible to take along an ice axe, and to know how to use it.

Camping, Huts, Hotels

One day you will be overcome by fatigue, the weather, or just the desire for creature comforts. The hotel is the answer. Small, reasonably priced hotels can be found in France, Italy, and Yugoslavia, but you must look around for them, and reservations are often necessary in high season. In Austria and Switzerland, many people rent rooms in their homes, with breakfast included in the price. Rates are usually more reasonable than those in the palatial hotels where Whymper and Mallory planned their fabulous trips.

If you are going on day hikes, it's best to try to find a centrally located campground. These are readily available throughout the Alps with the exception of the Italian Dolomites, where campgrounds are often 50 km or more from the trailheads. Once you have

Hut keeper at Cabane de Valsorey (Hike No. 20)

exhausted the hikes accessible from the campground, move on to another region, country, or mountain range. European campgrounds are well equipped with hot and cold running water, showers, sensible regulations—and lots of people during the summer months.

A great deal has been written about the European mountain hut system. It is quite possible to travel from France to Yugoslavia and stay in huts all along the way. Most of these huts, constructed of wood, stone, and corrugated iron, are operated by mountaineering clubs; some are private. They are almost always strategically placed, at intervals of 4 to 6 hours' hiking time. During the summer months, they are looked after by a sunburned hutkeeper (or his wife) who is usually a short-order cook and an aspiring mountain guide. Many huts serve hot meals and snacks and provide bunk-style lodging. They are never cheap; if you are going to stay in more than two or three of them, it is worth joining an Alpine club and benefitting from the members' discount. The main offices of Alpine clubs are in major cities, often far from the mountains. Addresses for these offices are listed at the back of this book. In many popular hiking areas, there are sections or branches of the clubs. The clubs can give you information about whether you need reservations for huts along your route, and how to make them. The huts provide shelter and fraternity. Most important, they make it possible to travel with a relatively light pack.

During my years in the Alps I've stayed in many of these huts. They are wonderful protection in a storm, but I've yet to catch up on all the nights' sleep I've lost. Someone is always snoring, sneezing, singing, smoking, or getting up at 1:00 a.m. to start a climb. In season, the huts are overcrowded and often unbearable. Still, a trip to the Alps isn't worth a schnitzl if you haven't tried a hut at least once.

I prefer—and recommend to you—a tent, a bubbling stream around the rise, and a view toward the east. That way the sun hits you early. Once you get above the tree line you can camp almost anywhere in the Alps, except in some of the national parks. There are, of course, other exceptions, and if you think you may be infringing on someone's rights, it's always a good idea to ask for permission to camp. If you can't speak the local language, point to your tent, then see what happens. In any case, most of the time you will put up your tent in the afternoon and pull it down the next morning; so it's more like bivouacking than camping. You'll be alone with the cows, sheep, goats, marmots, chamois, ibex, flies, mosquitoes, and the elements. Using a tent gives you marvelous mobility and that delightful sense that you are really free. You can stop where and when you want; all you need is a strong back. Many of our day hikes can easily be combined into overnight trips and we indicate this in the descriptions.

Food, Water, Maps

One of the joys of hiking in the Alps is that you are never more than a day or so from a mountain village. Even on the long traverse of the Pyrenees, or the high route, finding fresh food involves just a hike down to a valley store, a nearby farm, or a restaurant. There you can eat, for quality and quantity, such mountain specialties as fondue au fromage, raclette, bauernschmaus, truites aux amandes, carbonara, or polenta; drink the local wines; and go on hiking if you are still able.

Since there are a lot of animals grazing in the mountains during the summer months, it's a good idea to avoid drinking stream water and to make the most of local wines. If you must drink water (and you certainly need it for cooking), fill your bottles from sure sources like the village fountain, a farm, a campground, or a source above a hut or refuge. If you must take water from a stream, you can boil it and hope for the best.

Cabane de Valsorey (Hike No. 20)

So-called purification kits are ineffective against certain micro-organisms. If used properly, iodine is said to be an effective water purifier; but then you might just as well drink beer or wine.

Each hike description contains the name of the relevant map and its publisher. While it is a good idea to buy these maps ahead of time at a bookstore or at the office of an Alpine club in a large city, they can also be bought in small villages near trailheads at some photo shops, souvenir stands, and, in Switzerland, in railroad stations. Most contour maps are on a scale of 1:50,000; but some are more precise at 1:25,000, which means 1 centimeter on the map equals 250 meters on the ground. The spelling of all place names in this book is taken directly from the recommended map(s) for each hike. In border areas, there may be variations in the spelling of place names.

For difficult or sustained hikes, free trail information and weather reports can be obtained from local guides' bureaus and tourist offices. If you are up in the mountains and passing a hut, you can always ask the hutkeeper about weather reports and trail conditions. You can also stop and ask farmers, shepherds, or other hikers and climbers. Europeans are proud of the fact that they can converse in several languages, even if not fluently, so you should have little trouble making yourself understood.

Pollution

Leave your camp cleaner than you found it. Carry out trash, tin cans, and garbage in plastic bags. Alpine clubs and nature organizations in the Alps have finally launched serious anti-pollution campaigns. As a result, within the past few years the high passes, favorite camping and picnic sites, and even the refuges (huts) are cleaner and more agreeable. You are a guest in another country; remember to treat your surroundings with respect.

Distances

In the Alps, trail signs indicate estimated hiking times, never distances; so depending on where you are, signs will say "H2, m30," "Std 2, min 30," or just "2.30" — meaning 2 hours and 30 minutes is the estimated hiking time. These estimates should be an average hiker's time; but what is "average"? In some cases, a hutkeeper or restaurant owner will underestimate hiking times in order to encourage hikers to climb to his place of business. Consequently, in this book we have used our hiking times. But keep in mind that Ira Spring and I are in our fifties and your time will vary according to your hiking speed, weather and trail conditions, and the composition of your party. We have tried to measure trail distances on the various maps, but with numerous switchbacks and steep ups and downs, this cannot be done accurately. So many of the distances are estimates which we have rounded off to the nearest ¼ or ½ kilometer or mile.

Landmarks

In contrast to the rapid turnover in ownership or names of American establishments, restaurants and hotels in the Alps are reliable landmarks—often the only reliable landmarks; a hotel or restaurant may have been in the same location, with the same name, for 50 or 100 years. Nevertheless, the publishers must point out that this is by no means a hotel or restaurant guide to the Alps, and mention of these places is not intended as an endorsement of one or another of them.

* * * *

As I noted, hiking in the Alps is marvelously varied. Many of our descriptions point out the peculiarities in each country or region. But while differences are readily apparent, similarities are not quite so obvious. I'm referring to the people who live in the mountains. Although sometimes reticent, mountain folk wherever they live are almost always friendly. From June until October (the best hiking season), they are up in the alpages (mountain pastures), farming and grazing their sheep, cows, and goats. They send their milk down into the valleys or prepare cheese for the coming winter. Some tend hotels or huts or have turned their barns into rural hostels; they welcome backpackers with pleasure. They are living on their land in their country, and as foreigners we must respect the countries, the people, and their customs. Even though you are just passing through, your contact with them can be worthwhile. Your visit frequently offers them a pleasant respite from the hard physical work that never ends. Communication of basic needs and ideas is always possible. If you don't speak the local tongue, try out your acting skills. The people may shake with laughter, but you will have communicated.

— Harvey Edwards

TABLE OF CONTENTS

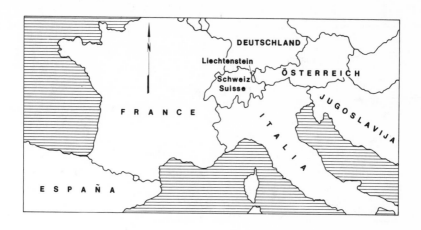

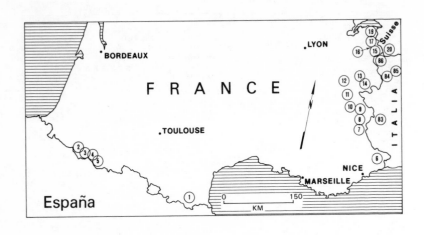

Chamonix Needles and Mer de Glace Glacier from trail to Lac Blanc (Hike No. 15)

FRANCE

1 GR 10, THE PYRENEES TRAVERSE   Traverse of the Pyrenees Range from the Atlantic to the Mediterranean; 700 km. Trips for a day, a week, or a summer.

2 THE TOUR OF THE PIC DU MIDI D'OSSAU   In Pyrenees National Park, a 2-day loop around a spectacular peak. Near Pau.

3 MASSIF VIGNEMALE   Valley walk in the Pyrenees; 1-4 days. Near Lourdes.

4 CIRQUE DE GAVARNIE   Short hike to a magnificent cirque in the Pyrenees. Near Lourdes.

5 RESERVE NATURELLE DE NEOUVIELLE   Day hikes among lakes and reservoirs in the Pyrenees. Near Lourdes.

6 THE PREHISTORIC PICTOGRAPHS OF MONT BEGO   Alpine lakes and ancient pictographs highlight 2-day hike. Near Nice.

7 FOUILLOUZE (REFUGE DE CHAMBEYRON)   Day and overnight hikes to a viewpoint and lakes. Near Guillestre.

8 TETE DE GIRARDIN   Tiny mountain-top chapel reached in day hike to a high pass; and 2-day loop from the pass.

9 CHATEAU-QUEYRAS   Starting at a picturesque castle near Guillestre, day hike or 2-day loop.

10 LAC DE L'EYCHAUDA, ECRINS NATIONAL PARK   Short, steep, 1-day climb to a barren lake below a small glacier. Near Briancon.

11 VENEON TORRENT, ECRINS NATIONAL PARK   Day hike or 2-day loop, beside a raging stream. Near Chambery.

12 COL DE LA PRA   Hike among alpine lakes, 1-2 days. Near Grenoble.

13 COL DE LA VANOISE, VANOISE NATIONAL PARK   Loop trip around the Vanoise Needle, with mountain meadows, lakes, and streams; 1 day. Near Albertville.

14 VANOISE GLACIER TRAVERSE, VANOISE NATIONAL PARK   High trail loop trip beneath the many tongues of the Vanoise Glacier; 3 days. Near Modane.

15 LAC BLANC   Day hike from Chamonix to two beautiful lakes and breathtaking views of the Chamonix Needles and Mont Blanc.

16 LACS NOIRS AND CORNU   From Chamonix, day hike to lakes and superb views of Mont Blanc.

17 THE CHAMONIX NEEDLES TRAVERSE   Long day hike from Chamonix to alpine meadows below towering spires.

18 LE TOUR DU MONT BLANC (TMB)   Loop trip around Mont Blanc, passing through a corner of Italy and Switzerland; 10 days, 160 km.

19 GR 5 (GRANDE RANDONNEE 5)   Trek from Lake Geneva to the Mediterranean; 575 km. Hike in week-long sections or spend a summer.

24 LA HAUTE ROUTE   Moderate-elevation traverse, 180 km, from Chamonix to Zermatt; 10 days or more.

83 TOUR AROUND MONT VISO   Loop trip around Mont Viso on the French-Italian border, with valleys, forests, streams, lakes, and flowers; 3 days. Reached from Torino in Italy or Guillestre in France.

1 GR 10 (GRANDE RANDONNEE 10)
The Pyrenees Traverse

One way 700 km, about 450 miles
Hiking time 6-8 weeks

As noted in the Introduction, the Pyrenees are not technically part of the Alpine system. This 400-km chain of mountains between France and Spain differs from the Alps in that summits are lower, but passes are higher and larger. There are far fewer glaciers, and they are smaller than glaciers in the Alps.

Although the Grande Randonnee 10 (better known as GR 10) trail is not as well known as the more popular GR 5 trail from Lake Geneva to Nice, it has a great deal to offer. It would be hard to say which of the two is more beautiful. The GR 10 starts at the town of Banyuls on the Mediterranean Sea and winds through valleys and across ridgetops for 700 km to Hendaye near the Atlantic Ocean. Most of the way it runs through forest and alpine pastures. Wildflowers abound at all levels and songbirds are especially noticeable. The trail crosses the Pyrenees National Park where you can see animals such as isards (similar to the chamois) and marmots. If you are lucky, you may see one of the thirty remaining brown bears in Europe.

Main trail junctions are fairly well marked, but much remains to be done on secondary trails. There are numerous road crossings and villages along the way, and occasionally the route follows a road. Mountain huts are strategically located, but most hikers carry substantial camping gear. The trail is well documented in a series of four small guidebooks published by the Comite National des Sentiers de Grande Randonnee, 92 rue de Clignancourt, 75883 Paris Cedex 18. Although the books are only in French, there are sufficient maps and charts so that non-French-speaking backpackers can understand the essentials.

It takes 6-8 weeks of steady hiking to traverse the range, a period of time few hikers have at their disposal. Thus, many backpackers satisfy their wanderlust by hiking the best parts of the route for a week or two each year. Since there are many access points, it is easy to take short hikes or hikes of 2-3 days, using buses to return to the starting point.

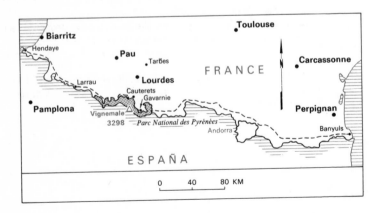

Massif Vignemale and Lac de Gaube

Several sections of the trail served by public transportation are: the 3-day trip from Merens-les Vals reached by highway N 20 to Siguer with views varying from pastoral to mountainous; the spectacular 2-day trip from Gavarnie to Cauterets under Mont Vignemale (Hike No. 3); and the 3-day hike from Arrens past the Refuge d'Ayous and its beautiful alpine lakes to the town of Etsaut (Hike No. 2).

2 THE TOUR OF THE PIC DU MIDI D'OSSAU

Round trip 17 km, 10½ miles
Hiking time 2 days
High point 2194 meters, 7196 feet
Elevation gain 900 meters, 2952 feet
Map IGN Parc National des Pyrenees 1

The French claim that the views of the Pic du Midi d'Ossau are extraordinary. They also claim that the double-pointed summit can be seen from a hundred different angles as the hiker loops around this 2884-meter peak. They may be right, but the 2 days we spent there in the fog and rain provided us with only one fleeting glimpse of the summit and the sight of three 70-year-old French hikers with black umbrellas emerging from the fog singing *Carmen*.

Instead of trying for the sensational by bucking intolerable weather, we should have selected the shorter loop trip via the Refuge d'Ayous. Three photogenic lakes are the goal on this lower hike. However, we had made our choice. Once we accepted the limited views and the drops of rain seeping through our hoods and down our necks, there were definite compensations: we saw many birds at lower elevations and higher up we traversed a garden of wildflowers, including daffodils in bloom. Near the Lac de Peyreget there was a field of alpine rose that, if not flooded out, would probably bloom in July.

From Pau follow N 134 south about 6 km, then turn left onto N 134B, marked "Col de Pourtalet," passing Laruns on the way to Gabas. At Gabas turn right onto D 231 to Lac de Bious-Artigues (a reservoir) and the road's end at 1417 meters.

The loop can be made in either direction; we went counterclockwise. Start out on the GR 10 along the lake shore, then climb beside a torrent. The trail crosses the river and at 2 km reaches a junction. The GR 10 heads for the Refuge d'Ayous and the three alpine lakes. If it is rainy and foggy, you might just as well go to the refuge; but if you are lucky enough to have good weather, go over the bridge and cross a huge, flat green valley.

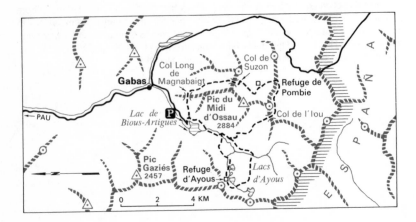

Pic du Midi d'Ossau from Lac de Bious-Artigues

Just short of 3 km you reach another junction. Straight ahead is the return section of the loop trail to the lakes; so turn left. Soon the trail starts climbing. It is excellent but steep as it switchbacks up to the 2194-meter-high Col de l'Iou at 6 km. From here you can enjoy the panorama of the Cirque d'Aneou and the faraway mountains that line the border between France and Spain.

With some ups and downs, the trail contours under Pic Peyreget and at 8 km reaches another junction. Keep left again, dropping slightly to the Refuge de Pombie at 9 km, elevation 2031 meters, hiking time 5½ hours. This is a good place to rest or, better still, spend the night.

From the refuge the trail crosses a boulder field and in 3 km climbs to the Col de Suzon, elevation 2127 meters, then down to the Col Long de Magnabaigt at 6½ km, elevation 1698 meters. It's 9 km (3 hours' walk) back to the start.

3 MASSIF VIGNEMALE

Round trip to Refuge des Oulettes 14 km, 9 miles
Hiking time 6 hours
High point 2151 meters, 6986 feet
Elevation gain 650 meters, 2132 feet

Refuge Bayssellance 26 km, 16 miles
Hiking time 13 hours; 2-3 days
High point 2734 meters, 8970 feet
Elevation gain 1238 meters, 4062 feet
Map IGN Parc National des Pyrenees 3

This hike through a V-shaped valley on the GR 10 trail, brings you to the foot of Mont Vignemale, 3298 meters, the highest peak in the Pyrenees National Park. You can continue on the same trail over a 2734-meter pass to the Refuge Bayssellance with its views of the largest glaciers in the Pyrenees. From this refuge, visit alpine lakes or continue on the GR 10 to Gavarnie. The trail is rough but the views are tremendous. We saw an isard.

By bus or auto from Tarbes, go to the resort town of Cauterets and from there continue 8 km to the Pont d'Espagne and the trailhead, elevation 1496 meters. By taking the chair lift you avoid a 200-meter climb; we preferred to walk this section of the GR 10.

The trail follows within sound of a rushing torrent and in 2 km reaches the Lac de Gaube, elevation 1725 meters, from which there is a post card view of the Vignemale massif. Follow the trail around the right side of the lake, crossing the stream, then climb past several roaring cascades. You will know you are only about 1 km from shelter when the valley flattens out into a huge green meadow and ends with a short climb to the Refuge des Oulettes at 7 km, elevation 2151 meters, approximately 3 hours from the road. This makes a satisfactory day hike.

Backpackers with more time will want to follow GR 10 to Refuge Bayssellance at 2651 meters, highest in the Pyrenees, and, because of snow conditions, not open until July 1. The trail, which climbs over the rocky Hourquette d'Ossoue (pass) at 1734 meters, is at

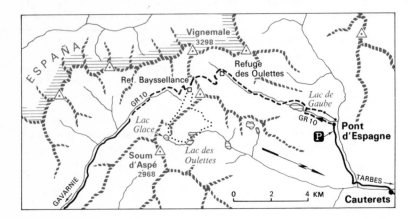

Mont Vignemale

least 6 km long. From Refuge Bayssellance, Lac Glace and Lac des Oulettes are attainable on a poorly defined trail either in day trips from the Refuge Bayssellance or as stops on a long alternate and rocky route back to the Refuge des Oulettes.

4 CIRQUE DE GAVARNIE

Round trip to viewpoint 7 km, 4 miles
Hiking time 3 hours
High point 1670 meters, 5479 feet
Elevation gain 300 meters, 984 feet
Map IGN Parc National des Pyrenees 3

This is one of the most photographed scenes in the Pyrenees Range. In spite of the throngs of tourists, the many horses on the trail, and the short distance involved, the hike to the cirque is an inspiring trip.

By auto or bus from Tarbes go past Lourdes to the town of Gavarnie on road N 21. Even from the parking area at the far end of town, elevation 1374 meters, the views are impressive.

The trail is easy to find. If the signs are missing, follow the horse tracks upstream. The horses stop at the Hotellerie du Cirque, elevation 1570 meters, 3 km from Gavarnie. Continue up the trail a few meters farther. At this point you enter a huge amphitheater of towering cliffs and silvery waterfalls. High above the cliffs are 3000-meter peaks with small glaciers, the source of the waterfalls and of the perpetual snow cone at the foot of the cliff.

To get away from the crowds, cross the river on a footbridge and climb a badly eroded trail up the steep green hillside opposite the hotel. After 100 meters you reach a green meadow. From a small knoll to the right, there is an aerial view of Gavarnie. From a small knoll to the left, there is a glorious view of the cirque. While sitting there we marvelled at the grace of two huge vultures with wingspreads of about 2 meters.

On the way back, for a change of scenery, pick up the trail to the Col de Vac which starts directly behind the Hotellerie du Cirque, climbing 200 meters in 2½ km to the col. Then make a short detour to the Plateau de Pailla, return to the col, and head back down to Gavarnie.

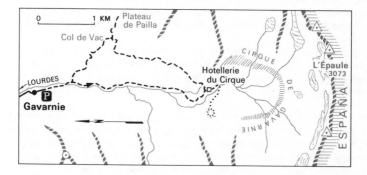

Cirque de Gavarnie

5 RESERVE NATURELLE DE NEOUVIELLE

Hiking time Lacs de Bastanet 2½ hours one way
Hiking time Lac de Port-Bielh 4 hours one way
Hiking time Lac de L'Ile 1 hour one way
Hiking time Lac de L'Oule 3 hours to 3 days
Map IGN Parc National des Pyrenees 4

Although this reserve is only 7 km long, it has many good hikes, flowers, wildlife, and lakes. It's a great wandering area, with trailheads better marked than junctions or trails themselves. The IGN map is a necessity. Since a secondary road penetrates the reserve, several high country lakes are easily reached by car. But it is more enjoyable to explore on foot. The only tent camping permitted in the reserve is in a designated area near Lac d'Aubert. However, there are several small shelters and refuges in and on the outskirts of the park.

The area is reached from highway N 117 between Toulouse and Tarbes; near Lannemezan head south, pass through the resort town of St. Lary on highway D 929 toward Cap-de-Long. At 16 km from St. Lary, you pass the trailhead to Lac de L'Oule; at 20 km turn right to Lac d'Oredon; and at 26 km, you reach the camping area, elevation 2190 meters.

To start exploring the lakes, try the hike from Lac d'Aumar over the Col d'Aumar to Lac de L'Ile, 2 km, 180 vertical meters. For a more ambitious hike, follow the GR 10 across the Col de Madamete and visit some of the lakes in the reserve's northern sector. A third possibility is to take the trail to Lac de L'Oule, hike around this giant reservoir to its inlet, and then follow the trail to Lacs de Milieu, about 7 km, elevation gain 750 meters. If tired, you can camp near the Refuge de Bastanet (a building owned by a power company); the next day, hike 6 km over the Col de Bastanet to Lac de Port-Bielh and loop back along the Rou de Port-Bielh to Lac de L'Oule.

The reserve is also an excellent place for relatively easy mountain climbing. Trails lead to the Pic d'Estibere and the Pic d'Anglade, which are over 2500 meters.

Lac de L'Oule

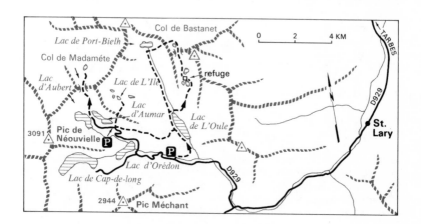

FRANCE

6 THE PREHISTORIC PICTOGRAPHS OF MONT BEGO

To the pictographs:
Round trip 16 km, 10 miles
Hiking time 7 hours
High point 2300 meters, 7546 feet
Elevation gain 900 meters, 2952 feet

Loop trip:
Round trip 26 km, 16 miles
Hiking time 2 days
High point 2549 meters, 8363 feet
Elevation gain 1150 meters, 3772 feet
Map D&R Haut Pays Nicois

Refuge des Merveilles and
Lac Long

The trail around Mont Bego in the Maritime Alps provides one of the most interesting 2-day loop trips we know. The trail, more than 2000 years old, passes through forest and meadows up to barren hills, chains of lakes, and prehistoric pictographs in the Vallee des Merveilles. This area is both an archeological reserve and a national park. The best trip is the 2-day loop; but a day hike to the lakes or a very long day hike to the pictographs located in a high desolate valley is also possible.

No one knows exactly how old the pictographs are or which tribes made them. Since many of the rocks were polished by ancient, long-gone glaciers, the carvings were certainly made after the Ice Age. Were the tribes sheep herders who escaped the Roman occupation by living in remote valleys; or were they earlier peaceful people who hid in these high valleys to avoid combat? The atmosphere is strange, and this beautiful barren spot encourages speculation and contemplation.

The Vallee des Merveilles or Mont Bego region is reached from Nice by train and bus, or by car over one of the most tortuous roads in France. If you are driving, from Nice follow D 2204, marked "Sospel" and "Frontier, Col de Tende," to the village of St.

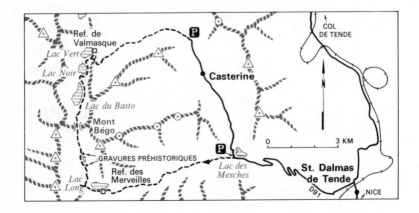

Pictographs in Vallee des Merveilles

Dalmas-de-Tende. From there pick up D 91, going toward Lac de Mesches and Casterine, for 9½ km to a parking place above the lake, elevation 1390 meters. If you plan to take the loop trip or explore the pictographs, park here. But if you are going just to the lakes, continue up the road another 4 km to Casterine where the pavement ends. Then follow the rough but manageable road another 2 km to the trailhead, elevation 1732 meters.

From the parking area on Lac des Mesches, walk back a few meters and find a narrow, rough road; follow it for 6 km to the Refuge des Merveilles on the side of Lac Long, elevation 2111 meters. From the refuge follow a well marked but unsigned trail around the west side of the lake to the junction at the far end. Take the right-hand trail toward the rushing stream. It climbs up and down beside the torrent into the Vallee des Merveilles to a high point above a tiny lake, 8 km from the road, elevation 2300 meters. Here you have to search for the pictographs among the rocks and boulders. Most are small and faint, cut into the smooth sides of the reddish-grey rock. Some are simple figures; others are more complicated figures and symbols. One can spend hours or even days studying this mysterious world.

The trail drops down to lake level, follows the river upstream, then with a series of switchbacks heads up over a 2549-meter col at 10 km. Then the trail switchbacks down to Lac du Basto, Lac Noir, and finally Lac Vert and the Refuge de Valmasque, elevation 2221 meters. It's a good haul from there back to the trailhead, so you will want to rest before returning.

7 FOUILLOUZE (REFUGE DE CHAMBEYRON)

Round trip to refuge 10 km, 6 miles
Hiking time 4½ hours
High point 2835 meters, 9302 feet
Elevation gain 750 meters, 2460 feet

Round trip to Tete de l'Homme 10 km, 6 miles
Hiking time 4 hours
High point 2455 meters, 8055 feet
Elevation gain 580 meters, 1902 feet
Map D&R Massifs du Queyras et Haute Ubaye

One short leg of the GR 5 trail (Hike No. 19) is a climb from the hamlet of Fouillouze to the Refuge de Chambeyron for a closeup view of the Brec de Chambeyron. The area around Fouillouze abounds in fascinating hiking, including trails up to the Col du Vallone and the Tete de l'Homme.

Fouillouze is in the Ubaye region. From highway 94 between Briancon and Gap, go to Guillestre and then south on road N 202-D 902 to the small town of St. Paul. This is about the last place to purchase groceries. From there follow the signs past Grand Serenne, and at 4 km turn right on a rough dirt road marked "Fouillouze." In a short distance cross a one-lane stone bridge over an awesome canyon through which runs the Ubaye (river). At 7½ km from St. Paul, you reach the hamlet of Fouillouze, elevation 1911 meters. A primitive campground is on the far side of town, but the hamlet also has a well equipped gite d'etape (rural hostel) and a restaurant or two.

The high lakes trip (via Refuge de Chambeyron) should not be attempted unless most of the snow has melted; other hikes in this area can be made in early summer, but are most impressive in autumn when the larch forests have turned golden.

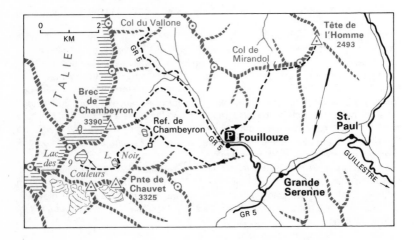

Pointe du Chauvet from trail to Tete de l'Homme

All hikes start from Fouillouze. Climb up to the refuge, elevation 2650 meters, and stay overnight; the next day hike over the schist and rubble rock past Lac Noir to Lac des Neuf Couleurs, 3 km from the refuge, 100 vertical meters. It is claimed that at certain times of day nine colors can be distinguished in this 2813-meter-high lake beneath the Brec de Chambeyron. Return by the same route or, for variety, cross over the Pas de la Couleta to the valley.

A second hike follows the GR 5 trail (Hike No. 19) on a narrow road by the campground, then continues on a wide path to the Col du Vallone, which is very close to the Italian border. For the Tete de l'Homme hike, walk to the campground and cross the stream on a bridge; a few meters farther, pick up a trail which rises steeply to the edge of the forest and an unmarked junction. Go right, following the trail through a larch forest to a high meadow and a superb view of the Pointe du Chauvet and the other Chambeyron spires. From the viewpoint, the trail becomes flat. First it contours around the hillside; then it climbs to the Col de Mirandol. Follow the ups and downs of the ridge to the summit, elevation 2455 meters, for a vertical gain of 580 meters. Return to Fouillouze by the same trail.

27

8 TETE DE GIRARDIN

Day hike:
Round trip 13 km, 8 miles
Hiking time 6 hours
High point 2870 meters, 9414 feet
Elevation gain 1120 meters, 3674 feet

Overnight loop trip: 22¾ km, 14½ miles
Hiking time 2 days
High point 2706 meters, 8878 feet
Elevation gain 2070 meters, 6790 feet
Map D&R Massifs du Queyras & Haute Ubaye

Hike to a tiny chapel on the 2870-meter summit of the Tete de Girardin for superb views of the rugged spires of the Pic de la Font Sancte, the massive range of the Aiguille de Chambeyron, and endless mountains and valleys. This can be a day hike or part of a 2-day loop. There are three trailheads from which you can begin, and the trails go to the same place. We selected the most scenic one.

From highway N 94 between Gap and Briancon turn east to Guillestre, then continue east, following N 202, marked "Col d'Izoard." At about 5½ km from Guillestre, turn right on road D 440 to the resort town of Ceillac. From there continue up the valley 3½ km to a group of farmhouses and the trailhead (with very limited parking), elevation 1750 meters.

The trail starts in forest as a wide wagon road then crosses under ski lifts on graded ski runs. Magnificent peaks tower above the trail. In 2 km the trail joins the GR 5 and continues onto a 2400-meter-high viewpoint. A bit farther is Lac St. Anne, situated at 2409 meters in a bowl without an outlet. From the lake, located 4 km from the trailhead, the route heads up and at 5½ km it reaches the 2706-meter-high Col Girardin. Climb the eastern slope to the round dome of the Tete de Girardin, 2870 meters, 6½ km from the road. The scenery and chapel may help you contemplate other worldly things; but when you get down to earth again you might reflect on what was involved in carrying the materials up to this majestic summit to construct the chapel.

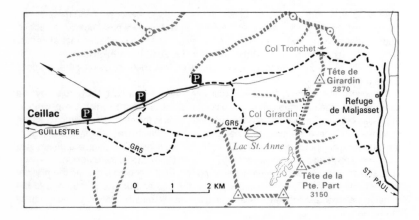

Brec de Chambeyron from Col Girardin

For backpackers who want to hike the 2-day loop, drop down from the col to the lovely stone Refuge de Maljasset at 1916 meters, a distance of approximately 5 km. The next day follow the road upstream ¾ km and then climb the grueling 5 km over rubble track through the 2658-meter-high Col Tronchet. Your reward as you climb will be wider and wider views. From the col it's another 6½ km to the starting point near Ceillac.

Chateau-Queyras

9 CHATEAU-QUEYRAS

Round trip 14 km, 9 miles
Hiking time 6 hours
High point 2200 meters, 7216 feet
Elevation gain 1000 meters, 3280 feet
Map D&R Massifs du Queyras & Haute Ubaye

This loop hike begins and ends at one of the most picturesque fortified cities in the French Alps. It can be walked in 1 day or extended to several days.

To reach the town of Chateau-Queyras, follow the directions in Hike No. 8 (Tete de Girardin), passing Guillestre and then following road N 202 which becomes N 547. Park just before reaching the town, elevation 1350 meters. Walk back down the road several hundred meters, and near the sign indicating the town of Chateau-Queyras you will find the GR 5 trail marked "Lac de Roue." The trail climbs steadily up a steep forested hillside, with endless short switchbacks and occasional glimpses of the white stone chateau below. At approximately 2 km, elevation 1800 meters, the steepness ends abruptly. A slight detour is enjoyable here. Follow signs which point to the Belvedere, where there are two excellent viewpoints: from the first you look back at the chateau and from the second into a deep valley. Rejoin the main trail and climb to the 1839-meter high Lac de Roue. Circle the lake until you reach a dirt road where you leave the GR 5 trail and turn right onto the GR 58. This follows the dirt road, and soon brings you to fine views of the sawtooth ridge of the Cote Belle Crete des Oules punctuating the horizon. Proceed to picturesque Souliers at 4 km, elevation about 1700 meters, where there is a gite d'etape (hostel) in case you are tired and hungry.

At the edge of Souliers find the GR 58 sign marked "Aiguilles." Follow this trail up a green shoulder of a ridge to 2200 meters, then contour around a steep hillside and descend into the Grand Vallon de Peas to another road a 8 km, elevation 2078 meters. This is the dividing point between the short and long hikes. The short loop follows the road down the valley to Rouet at 12 km; then by trail it descends to Chateau-Queyras.

Although we have not hiked the longer loop, it appears to be a tour through delightfully green meadows. From the junction in the Grand Vallon de Peas, cross the river and follow GR 58 upstream, crossing the 2629-meter Col de Peas. Drop down and spend the night in the hostel at Les Fonts, elevation 2050 meters. The next day follow the trail beside the Torrent de Pierre for a 3-4 hours' climb to the Col de Malrif, elevation 2857 meters, and walk down to the town of Abries. From there it's a leisurely walk or bus ride back to the big stone chateau.

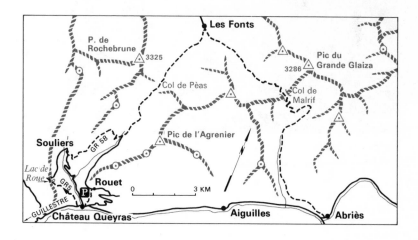

Lac de l'Eychauda

10 LAC DE L'EYCHAUDA
Ecrins National Park

Round trip 8 km, 5 miles
Hiking time 2½ hours up, 1½ down
High point 2512 meters, 8239 feet
Elevation gain 770 meters, 2526 feet
Map D&R Massifs Ecrins Haut Dauphine

Lac de l'Eychauda is an excellent example of a lake carved out of a mountain by a glacier. The rocks by its sides are polished and scratched by the movement of ice. The water is silt-grey, but unlike most glacial lakes, this one has no visible outlet despite all the water that flows into it from the Glacier de Seguret Foran and snow melt from the fields above.

Although the trail is in excellent condition, as are most of the popular routes in the French national parks, it is poorly marked. A good topographic map is necessary to help you locate trailheads and junctions, and for general orientation.

From Argentiere la Besse on highway N 94 south of Briancon, follow road N 94E to Vallouise; turn right on a narrow paved road marked "Les Choulieres." At 6 km the pavement ends. At 10½ km from Vallouise, the road is barred at the boundary of the national park. Because the final kilometer of road is rough and there is only limited parking, it is best to park earlier by a small creek at 9½ km, elevation 1742 meters.

From the parking place, hike 1½ km on the road, which ends at a farm. Then follow the steepening trail up the valley to a final series of switchbacks. At 4 km, elevation 2512 meters, the trail tops a rocky ridge. From there descend to the lake, which is only a few meters farther on. For a better view of the lake and the Glacier de Seguret Foran, go over the rocky knoll to the right and follow a well defined trail another kilometer, switchbacking to the top of the craggy rim surrounding the lake.

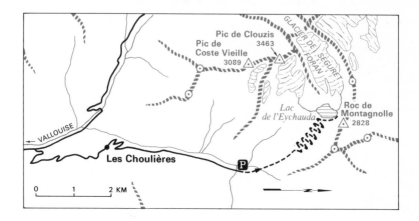

Trail to Refuge de la Pilatte

11 VENEON TORRENT
Ecrins National Park

Round trip 14 km, 9 miles
Hiking time 5 hours
High point 2200 meters, 7216 feet
Elevation gain 480 meters, 1574 feet
Map D&R Massifs Ecrins Haut Dauphine

This hike along a torrent to the snout of the Pilatte Glacier can easily be extended to 2 or 3 days. Trails are well maintained but poorly marked.

From highway N 91 near the town of Bourg d'Oisans, turn onto road D 530, and drive 26 tortuous km to the road's end at the village of La Berade, the center of a popular mountain climbing area, elevation 1720 meters. Park on the outskirts of town, walk through it on the main street, and then keep following what is now a trail upstream. At 3 km you pass the Refuge du Plan du Carrelet, a small restaurant. At 3½ km the trail forks. The right fork crosses the river, but do not take it—keep going straight ahead. At 4 km there is another fork and a possible side trip to the Refuge Temple Ecrins, which you can see high on a hill above the trail. Continue on the valley trail and at 7 km, elevation 2135 meters, cross the raging river on a precarious-looking bridge; climb a short distance above the river to an unmarked trail intersection.

The upstream trail offers a second possible side trip: climb over a rock slide and snow patches to the Refuge de la Pilatte on a knoll overlooking the Pilatte Glacier and a ring of craggy peaks. Although this side trip adds 2 hours of hiking and 450 meters of climbing, the refuge is a spectacular place to spend the night. Precisely because of that, you should get there early; it is a popular place with mountain climbers.

Back at the junction (near the river crossing), stay on the west side of the valley and follow that trail downstream in order to obtain different perspectives of the valley and mountains. This route is not recommended until the snow has completely melted from the steep couloirs that cross the trail. At about 10 km there is another unmarked trail junction. The upper way is the longer but more interesting way back, but it will add an extra hour and 200 meters of climbing. The shorter way follows a series of switchbacks to a footbridge and rejoins the east side trail only 3½ km from the road's end.

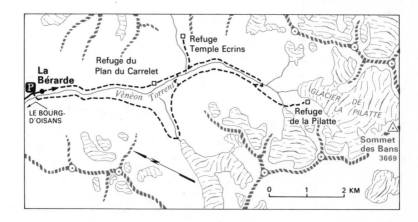

12 COL DE LA PRA

Round trip 8 km, 5 miles
Hiking time to refuge 3 hours
High point 2160 meters, 7087 feet
Elevation gain 840 meters, 2755 feet
Map D&R Chartreuse, Belledonne, Maurienne 4

Lakes, snow-covered peaks, and soft forest trails gave us our excuse for setting off for 2 or 3 days of enjoyable hiking near Grenoble. In most years, the snow and ice disappear from the lakes by July.

The easiest way to reach this area is by taking a bus to the ski resort of Chamrousse, where the downhill events were held at the 1968 Winter Olympic Games. However, we wanted to avoid tourist areas; consequently we chose the trail which left from Freydiere. From Grenoble travel by bus or car to the town of Domene. In the city center next to the PTT (Post Office), turn uphill and take the Revel-Freydiere road. After Revel continue past several junctions another 12 km to Freydiere, where you will find a restaurant. Climb straight ahead another 2½ km to the road's end and the trailhead, elevation 1320 meters.

The trail climbs steeply up a wooded ridge for 2 km, then contours for a while and leaves the timber to climb to Lac du Crozet, 4 km, elevation 1980 meters. It is a large lake with a small dam at one end. The trail circles the lake, climbs over the 2160-meter Col de la Pra, and continues a short distance to the Refuge de la Pra. Trail signs list the hiking time as 2½ hours; however, if you get there in 3 hours you are doing very well.

This comfortable refuge is an ideal base for walks to nearby lakes. To the south are Lac Longet and tiny Lac Leama; and 4 km farther, toward Chamrousse, one finds Lacs Robert. To the north, within easy distance, is Lac du Domenon. We expected the lakes to be surrounded by luscious rock gardens, flowers, and green meadows, but when we were there one July, after an unusually severe winter, a 3-meter carpet of snow covered everything.

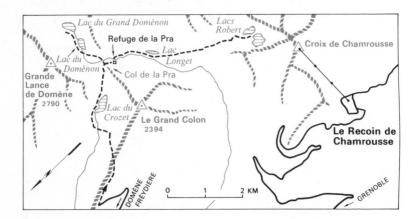

View from trail to Col de la Pra

Edelweiss

13 COL DE LA VANOISE
Vanoise National Park

Round trip 14 km, 9 miles
Hiking time 6 hours (7 hours for loop)
High point 2531 meters, 8304 feet
Elevation gain 890 meters, 2920 feet
Map D&R Parc National de la Vanoise

This marvelous loop trail circles the Aiguille de la Vanoise (the Vanoise spire) and goes up to the Col de la Vanoise. Besides splendid views of lakes and glaciers, one finds lush green meadows and many varieties of wildflowers including edelweiss. This can be an enjoyable day hike, or the starting point for many days of high-country backpacking in the Vanoise National Park.

Travel on highway 90 toward the Petit St. Bernard Pass to the city of Moutiers, then take route N 515 for 28 km to the village of Pralognan, which can also be reached by bus. If you want to save considerable energy, you can ride part of the way up this trip on the Mont Bochor telepherique (cable car), which you board at Pralognan. However, if you want to walk all the way, the trail begins at the tiny hamlet of Fontanette. Take the road on the north side of Pralognan for 2¾ km to Fontanette, elevation 1640 meters.

The trail is well marked and starts on a wide, graded ski piste (run), but after 1 km it leaves the ski trail and narrows and climbs steadily within sight of a cascading stream. At 2 km you pass the junction with the Mont Bochor trail (the route taken by those who rode the telepherique) and go under the spectacular north face of the Aiguille de la Vanoise. The trail makes a sharp bend around the needle-like aiguille, traverses the shores of Lac Long, which in late summer is virtually dry, to the Col de la Vanoise and the Refuge Felix Faure (or Refuge Col de la Vanoise), elevation 2531 meters. This is a fine place to relax and enjoy the views and flowers.

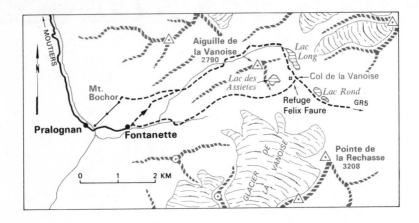

Refuge Felix Faure

At the refuge, the trail splits: straight ahead it goes to Lac Rond and extensive high-country trails (Hike No. 14) while the right fork traverses the south side of the Aiguille de la Vanoise and descends to the starting point at Fontanette. If you are in a hurry, descend on the same trail you came up. The return on the loop trail involves a delicate stream crossing, is steep, and consequently is less traveled. Experienced backpackers will derive much pleasure from this loop trail.

14 VANOISE GLACIER TRAVERSE
Vanoise National Park

Round trip 22 km, 14 miles
Hiking time 2 days
High point 2600 meters, 8528 feet
Elevation gain 1710 meters, 5609 feet
Map D&R National de la Vanoise

This loop trip high above the deep canyon of the Doron River in the Vanoise National Park is part of the 575-km, 357-mile GR 5 trail which runs from Lake Geneva to Nice (Hike No. 19). The trail winds below the numerous tongues of the 11-km-long Vanoise Glacier, then, crossing the river near its headwaters, returns on the opposite side of the canyon, offering grand views of glaciers, peaks, and the route just traveled.

From Chambery take highway N 6 toward Torino to the small village of Termignon east of Modane. At the village, follow a narrow paved road upstream about 2 km to a small parking area, elevation 1350 meters. Cross the river and walk upstream 100 meters on a farm road to the trail. It climbs unmercifully, 700 meters in 2½ km, to intersect the GR 5 at a cluster of farmhouses, elevation 2038 meters. Follow the GR 5 north with ups and downs and superb views of the valley and mountains. Reach the comfortable Refuge de l'Arpont at 5 km in approximately 3 hours. Drinks and lodging are available.

From the refuge, continue climbing to a 2600-meter-high point overlooking the Pelve Glacier. The trail descends almost 300 meters to a crossing of Letta stream. Then with more downs than ups, at 11 km you reach a junction. Keep right, descending rapidly to the valley bottom and a crossing of the Doron River, at 12½ km, elevation 2040 meters, after about 6 hours of steady hiking. Follow a farm road upstream 500 meters to a trail crossing. The left trail heads north 1 km to the Chalet Refuge d'Entre Deux Eaux, a good overnight stop. Try the reblochon cheese which is made at the farm next door by a family that spends its summer months there with their herd of cows.

Next day, go back to the intersection and follow the right trail heading south, climbing steeply to the Refuge Porte du Plan du Lac at 15 km, elevation 2380 meters. From here

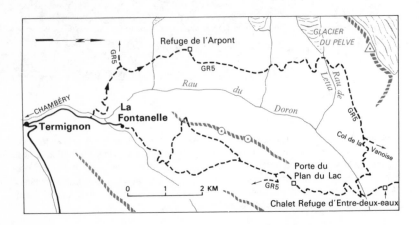

Farmhouse near Refuge de l'Arpont

the trail parallels a farm road on a relatively flat plateau; at the southern end, the road makes a series of long switchbacks while the trail drops steeply to the small town of La Fontanelle at 21½ km. From there it's just ½ km back to the starting point.

15 LAC BLANC

One way La Flegere mid-station to Lac Blanc-Col des Montets 10 km, 6 miles
Hiking time 4½ hours
High point 2352 meters, 7715 feet
Elevation gain 535 meters, 1755 feet
Map D&R Massif du Mont Blanc

An easy climb brings you to an alpine lake with a superb view of the Mont Blanc massif, the Chamonix needles, and the Mer de Glace Glacier. From the lake you can also enjoy the views of the Aiguille Verte and the Argentiere Glacier and then, by hiking along the mountain flanks, you can rejoin the highway at the Col des Montets.

From Chamonix at 1030 meters, pick up the trail to Lac Blanc next to Le Brevent tram station, then hike in a northerly direction toward La Flegere. The trail soon joins Le Petit Balcon—the flanking trail that runs the entire length of the valley—but then branches off to the left, climbing steeply through forest until it bursts out at the tree line at La Flegere, elevation 1817 meters, in about 3 hours. You can avoid this climb by taking the telepherique from Les Praz (up the valley from Chamonix) to La Flegere mid-station, or continue by taking the gondola lift to Index. In the first case, you hike down in a northerly direction into a large bowl, near a hotel occupied by French mountain troops, and then climb past the small Flegere Lake. The trail becomes progressively steep until it arrives at Lac Blanc, 2352 meters.

From Index, via the gondola, the traverse across to Lac Blanc may be slippery and spotted with snow except late in the summer. Follow the trail in a northeasterly direction into a large bowl called La Grande Combe des Aiguilles Crochues. From there, hike around a rock spire and make the long traverse which joins the trail coming up from La Flegere.

The views of the two lakes and the Mont Blanc massif, particularly at sunrise and sunset, are extraordinary, and many people stay overnight in the hut, which is on the lake shore. You can either retrace your steps to La Flegere tram station, or continue farther along the flanks of the valley to enjoy mountain views from many different angles.

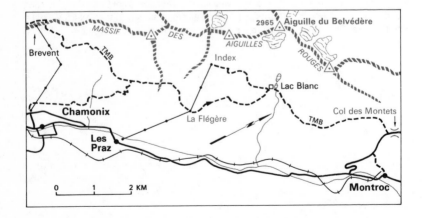

Chalet-hotel du Lac Blanc and Aiguille Verte

The trail starts to the left of the hut and generally follows the landscape's contours; after passing several small lakes, it arrives at the switchbacks which lead down to the Col des Montets. Catch a ride back to Chamonix or cut across to the hamlet of Montroc, 1 km away, where you can get a train to Chamonix.

16 LACS NOIRS AND CORNU

Round trip 9 km, 5½ miles
Hiking time 3½ hours
High point 2550 meters, 8364 feet
Elevation gain 600 meters, 1968 feet
Map D&R Massif du Mont Blanc, Beaufortin

Of the many hikes in and around Chamonix there are at least two that one should not miss: Lac Blanc (Hike No. 15) and Lacs Noirs and Cornu. These hikes provide magnificent views of the Mont Blanc massif from excellent vantage points. The great snow and rock peaks are often reflected in these high mountain lakes; however, after winters with heavy snow the lakes can remain icebound throughout the summer months. By traversing the Massif des Aiguilles Rouges all the way from the Col des Montets to Les Houches, you could combine both lake hikes in 1 day. However, that's a long distance, and there is no nearby shelter to use when the weather turns foul.

The excellent trail from Chamonix to Plan Praz climbs 1000 meters and takes about 3 hours; however, the Brevent cable car takes about 10 minutes, leaving you more time to explore and enjoy the lakes. Take your choice.

From the cable car station at Plan Praz, elevation 2000 meters, follow a graded ski trail to the left. In about 200 meters you walk under a ski lift to a three-way trail junction. The left trail goes to the Col du Brevent, the right one to La Flegere. Take the middle trail marked "Col du Lac Cornu." Although you will be interrupted by an occasional rock to scramble over as the trail climbs to the 2406-meter col, 3½ km from the cable car, the biggest hazard is not being able to concentrate on where you are going. The tremendous views of the Chamonix needles and Mont Blanc are distracting.

Drop over the col about 150 meters to Lac Cornu, a rather large lake carved out of the hillsides by ancient glaciers. You are above the tree line here, and the landscape is composed mostly of scrubby green bushes stashed between the rocks. To reach Lacs Noirs take a rough trail from the south side of Lac Cornu. It climbs around a hill and follows the outlet stream of Lacs Noirs, 2494 meters, 4½ km from Plan Praz. For the return trip, climb to the Col des Lacs Noirs and back along the ridge to the Col du Lac Cornu, then down to the cable car station at Plan Praz.

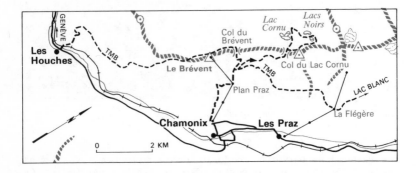

Mont Blanc from trail to Col du Lac Cornu

17 THE CHAMONIX NEEDLES TRAVERSE

One way 21 km, 13 miles
Hiking time 9 hours
High point 2204 meters, 7229 feet
Elevation gain 1300 meters, 4264 feet
Map D&R Massif du Mont Blanc

Chamonix Needles

The Chamonix needles (aiguilles) are impressive from the valley floor and even more so from across the valley. However, for a neck-stretching view and a good closeup impression of the granite rock which is such a favorite with mountain climbers, follow the trail that traverses directly under the needles. The deep gorge of the Mer de Glace (Sea of Ice) cuts the route in two so there is a lot of up and down hiking. Therefore, we felt justified in gaining our initial altitude by riding up the Telepherique des Grands Montets.

To get to the telepherique, take the bus or train to Argentiere and ride the tram to the middle station (Lognan), elevation 1950 meters. From there drop down a short way to a good trail that contours around the hillside through a mixture of meadows and forest, heading south towards Chamonix. For about 3 km the trail descends and then reaches a junction. Although both trails end up at more or less the same place, the left trail gives the best views. It descends a steep gully to the Chalet du Chapeau (drinks and snacks available) with head-on views of the Chamonix needles rising above the Mer de Glace as well as the valley all the way to Les Houches. On the way down you'll soon find a network of trails. Be sure to take the trail marked "Sentier Facile" (easy trail). Find a trail marked "Village des Bois" which cuts off to the left and finally leads to a trail going south through the forest. Take that and eventually turn left and cross the Arveyron (river) on the suspended bridge called the Pont Himalayen. Right after the bridge turn right, following the stream for a few meters, and turn left a short distance to the dirt road. About 30 meters downhill on your left is a steep trail called the Chemin de la Filia which goes up to the Fontaine de Caillet and Montenvers, elevation 1913 meters, about 11 km from Argentiere.

At Montenvers, after wading through the crowds of tourists, the inevitable post card/souvenir stands, and the zoo (which, unfortunately, imprisons mountain animals and birds), take the upper trail that climbs steeply over a 2204-meter ridge with stunning views of the Mer de Glace Glacier as well as the Aiguille de Charmoz. From the high point you then contour around a steep hillside with a seemingly vertical view straight

down the Chamonix Valley; then the trail joins the lower route coming up from Montenvers. From here, with more ups than downs, the trail traverses the Chamonix Valley and heads for the Plan de l'Aiguille. Although the full height of the needles is partially hidden by a moraine, the massiveness of the rock provides dramatic perspectives at each turn in the trail.

From the Plan de l'Aiguille you can ride the Aiguille du Midi cable car down to Chamonix, or hike down either on the Blaitiere trail or one of the two trails that leave directly from the telepherique station.

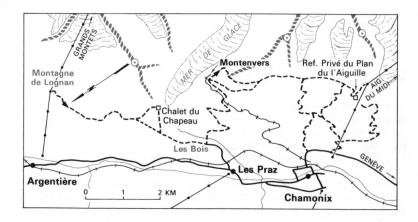

47

Les Grandes Jorasses from trail above Val Veni

18 LE TOUR DU MONT BLANC (TMB)

One way 160 km, about 100 miles
Hiking time 7-12 days
High point 2537 meters, 8321 feet
Elevation gain 7117 meters, 23,344 feet
Map D&R Massifs du Mont Blanc

At 4807 meters, Mont Blanc is the highest mountain in the Alps. The Tour du Mont Blanc (shown on most maps as TMB), or the trip around Mont Blanc, completely encircles the big white peak and its attendant mountains, famous peaks like the Aiguille du Midi, Les Grandes Jorasses, Mont Dolent. The trail skips in and out of France, Italy, and Switzerland, through six major valleys, over many moderately high alpine passes, through forests, and along rivers, roads, and trails. In good weather the alpine scenery has few equals anywhere in the world; and the huts, hotels, villages, and cities along the way make this 7- to 12-day hike one of the most popular jaunts in Europe. More than 10,000 people do it every year—4-year-old children and 75-year-old adults have hiked the trip with pleasure. Like any long loop hike, it requires time and pace, planning and patience.

You can start anywhere along the route. If the weather turns bad, you can wait it out in a cabin or stay in greater comfort in Chamonix, Courmayeur, or Champex hotels, eating truites aux amandes, fondue, or raclette in good restaurants. Once the weather clears, off you go again. Unless you choose some of the splendid variant routes, you won't be alone. The company you keep will no doubt be international. If you are bunking in the huts rather than camping, it's a good idea to telephone ahead for a reservation or at least to arrive before 3:00 p.m. Since this is a heavily traveled route, finding a place to put your tent requires a lot of discretion.

The main stages of the route, with suggested overnight stops indicated by an asterisk, are as follows:

1—Les Houches-Col de Voza-Les Contamines/Montjoie*

2—Les Contamines-Nant Borrant-La Balme-Col du Bonhomme-Refuge de la Col du Bonhomme*

3—Refuge de la Col du Bonhomme-Les Chapieux-La Ville des Glaciers-Col de la Seigne (Italy), 2516 meters-Refuge Elisabetta Soldini*

4—Refuge Elisabetta Soldini-Col Checroui (Hike No. 86)-Courmayeur*

5—Courmayeur-Val Sapin-Val Ferret-Arnuva-Grande Col Ferret (Hike No. 87), 2537 meters (Switzerland)-Ferret-Praz de Fort or Champex*

6—Champex-La Forclaz-Col de Balme (France), 2191 meters-Le Tour*

7—Le Tour-La Flegere-Plan Praz (Hike No. 15)-Le Brevent, 2525 meters-Merlet (Zoo)-Les Houches*

Several variant routes along the way, as well as aerial tramways, roads, buses, and taxis can shorten or lengthen this famous trip. Be prepared for a few days of bad weather, and plenty of views of high mountains and glaciers. For more details, see the recommended maps, and look for the trail marked TMB.

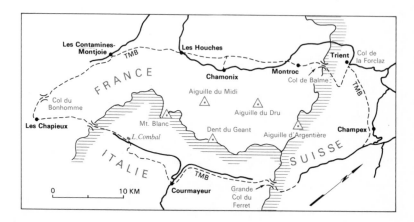

19 GR 5 (GRANDE RANDONNEE 5)

Length 575 km, about 360 miles
Hiking time 1-2 months
Maps IGN D&R Chablais, Faucigny & Genevois; Mont Blanc & Beaufortain; Parc National de la Vanoise; Haut Dauphine; Queyras & Haute Ubaye; Alpes de Provence; Haut Pays Nicois

The dream of many backpackers is to have sufficient time to traverse the French Alps from Lake Geneva (Lac Leman) to the Mediterranean Sea. It takes at least a month—without exploring variant routes or summit climbing along the way. Since most people don't have that much vacation time, they select a different section of the GR 5 each year, gradually making their way from north to south.

In fact, the GR 5 trail starts in flat Holland; but its most impressive section is in the French Alps. Starting from the lakeside village of St. Gingolf, the trail climbs rapidly into the mountains. It crosses high mountain saddles and pastures full of grazing cows; it passes small villages and ski areas like Sixt, Chamonix, Val d'Isere, Ceillac; it touches briefly the rail junction city of Modane and the walled Middle Ages city of Briancon. After skirting the Mont Blanc massif, the GR 5 goes through the Beaufortin, a province famous for its cheeses; the Vanoise National Park, where animals, glaciers, and high peaks are breathtaking; and the lovely Queyras region, a mixture of calm valleys and rocky paths. Then the GR 5 crosses into the southern Alps, skirting the French-Italian border, and drops through the Mercantour region where ancient tribes lived in stone caves thousands of years ago and left vestiges of their civilization carved in the rocks (Hike No. 6). Then the trail drops through hilltop villages dominated by church steeples down to the hustle-bustle cities of Nice or Menton on the Mediterranean Sea.

The GR 5 is one of the longest and most varied hikes in the Alps and is certainly the best designed. In the past 15 years its architects have worked to keep the trail away from big cities and located in the mountains, or at least on small secondary roads away from traffic. The organizations that manage the trail have registered more than 100 rural hostels, hotels, and mountain refuges, so that there is always a clean place to stay and friendly local people who welcome you into their homes for a drink, food, and good

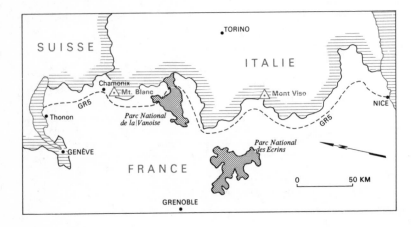

Pointe du Chauvet and chapel at Fouillouze

cheer. However, you can camp out all the way from Lake Geneva to the Mediterranean, except in the national park section.

The idea behind it all was to encourage young and old people—French as well as foreigners—to frequent the French Alps, thus helping the depressed mountain economy. The organizers worked with local inhabitants, helped them repair facilities in their villages, and financed an occasional gite d'etape (hostel). Thus they made the GR 5 one of the most popular hiking trails in the Alps. In wintertime, the traverse on skis is also feasible, but the route is from south to north.

Detailed information about the GR 5 can be obtained from the organization that supervises it. Write to CIMES, 14, rue de la Republique, 38027 Grenoble-Cedex, France.

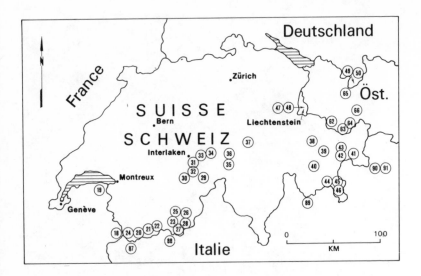

SWITZERLAND-SUISSE-SCHWEIZ

18   LE TOUR DU MONT BLANC (TMB)   Loop trip around Mont Blanc, passing through a corner of Italy and France; 10 days, 160 km.

20   CABANES DE VELAN AND DE VALSOREY   Hike to either of two mountain huts, 1-2 days; superb mountain and glacier views. Reached from the highway to Grand St. Bernard Pass.

21   LACS DE TSOFERAY   Small lakes and breathtaking view of the Grand Combin reached in a long day hike. Near Martigny.

22   AROLLA - THE LADDER TRAIL   Over a mountain pass and down a steel ladder, hike to the Cabane Dix; 1-2 days. Near Sion.

23   MEIDPASS   Steep, 1-day climb to alpine meadows and lakes, with views into the Rhone Valley. Near Sion.

24   LA HAUTE ROUTE   Moderate-elevation traverse, 180 km, from Chamonix to Zermatt; 10 days or more.

25   AUF KRINDELN, LOTSCHENTAL VALLEY   One of many short hikes from the valley; magnificent views. Near Sion.

26   TASCHHUTTE   Short hike, 1-2 days, to a mountain hut; views of the Weisshorn. Near Zermatt.

27   SCHONBIELHUTTE   Directly under the Matterhorn, hike beside a glacier; 1-2 days. Near Zermatt.

28   GORNERGRAT   Ride on a cog railroad to views of Monte Rosa and the Matterhorn, then a hike down for different perspectives of these peaks; 1 day. Near Zermatt.

29   GROSSER ALETSCH GLACIER   Ride a cable car to a view of the largest glacier in the Alps, then a hike through villages and farms to a lake for more views; 1 day. Near Brig.

30   OESCHINENSEE   One of the most photogenic lakes in Switzerland is the highlight of this day hike. Near Kandersteg.

Sheep grazing near the Bovel hut (Hike No. 46)

31 WENGEN Ride on a cog railroad to a station below the Eiger, then return by trail for views of the glacier-carved Lauterbrunnen Valley; 1 day. Near Interlaken.

32 OBERHORNSEE Steep trail in forest and meadows to a small lake surrounded by spectacular mountains; long day or overnight hike. Near Interlaken.

33 FAULHORN Traverse of a long ridge with views of villages, lakes, and glacier-clad mountains; 1 day. Near Interlaken.

34 GROSSE SCHEIDEGG Ride on a chair lift and then a long day hike through alpine farms to a small lake. Near Interlaken.

35 ALBERT HEIM HUTTE Day hike to a hut with commanding views of peaks and valleys, and return by a different trail. Near Furkapass.

36 CHELENALP HUTTE Hike around a mountain reservoir, then up a valley with a rushing stream and views of glaciers; 1-2 days. Near Andermatt.

37 GEMSFAIREN (KLAUSENPASS) Walk on a service road to an alpine farm, then by trail or wandering to higher views; half day or more. Near Klausenpass.

38 ALTEINSEE (AROSA) Day hike starting in forest, then passing several waterfalls en route to a lake surrounded by alpine meadows. Near Arosa.

39 FUORCLA DA GRIALETSCH Day hike to a small tarn and hut with views of mountains and glaciers. Near Davos.

40 VAL MULIX Forest and meadow hike on a seldom used trail to a pleasant mountain lake; 1 day. Near Albulapass.

41 ALP GRIMMELS, SWISS NATIONAL PARK Half-day hike on a short, steep trail to an alpine meadow heavily grazed by deer. Near Zernez.

42 ALP TRUPCHUN, SWISS NATIONAL PARK Valley hike from forest to alpine meadows famous for wildlife; 1 day. Near Zernez.

Chapel at Bettmeralp (Hike No. 29)

43 FUORCLA VAL SASSA, SWISS NATIONAL PARK   Traverse through the park, and a climb over a barren pass; 2 days. Near Zernez.
44 TSCHIERVA HUTTE   Starting in Pontresina, long day hike or easy 2-day hike to a hut overlooking the Tschierva Glacier and Piz Roseg.
45 PIZ LANGUARD   Trail hike to the top of a 3261-meter peak with dramatic views of Piz Bernina. The best place in Switzerland to see ibex, chamois, and marmots. Day hike, but recommended for 2 days. Starts in Pontresina.
46 MORTERATSCH GLACIER   Easy, 1-day trail hike beside a glacier to a hut with views of Piz Palu. Near Pontresina.

LIECHTENSTEIN

47 AUGSTENBERG   Loop trip to a high vantage point, 1-2 days. Near Vaduz.
48 HEUBUHL-RAPPENSTEIN RIDGE TRAIL   Day hike along a ridge crest overlooking the Rhine Valley. Near Vaduz.

Mont Velan and Cabane de Velan

20 CABANES DE VELAN AND DE VALSOREY

Round trip Cabane de Velan 14 km, 9 miles
Hiking time 7 hours round trip
High point 2569 meters, 8426 feet
Elevation gain 937 meters, 3073 feet
Maps Martigny 282, Arolla 283, Courmayeur 292, and Valpelline 293

The hiker has a choice of two huts, each with high dramatic views. The Cabane de Velan, perched on the flanks of Mont Velan, is by far the more popular of the two, with a great view of the Grand Combin, a glacier-shrouded mountain. The Cabane de Valsorey, underneath the Grand Combin, has an equally good view of Mont Velan, but reaching that hut is harder. One section of the trail is so difficult that we recommend it for experienced hikers only. For those capable of visiting both huts, overnight stays are a necessity.

The trail starts in the village of Bourg St. Pierre just off the Grand St. Bernard Pass highway, leaving either from the bus stop in the village or a parking area where the trail crosses the highway, elevation 1632 meters. The trail follows the left side of Valsorey stream, crossing a farm road at several points. At times the road is open to public travel, but it is very narrow, with virtually no room for passing or parking. At 2 km you pass a farmhouse and the road ends. At 4 km, boulder-hop a glacial stream, which can be difficult in late afternoon when it becomes a raging torrent. At 4½ km you reach an intersection: the left fork climbs to the Cabane de Valsorey; the right fork goes to the Cabane de Velan, which can be seen on a high ridge silhouetted against Mont Velan. The Cabane de Velan trail crosses Valsorey stream on a bridge and then switchbacks up a green slope to the hut, 7 km, elevation 2569 meters, located next to the Glacier du Tseudet.

If you choose the Cabane de Valsorey, keep on the left fork of the trail, climbing past abandoned farm buildings toward a tiny cleft in a fortress-like cliff that blocks all access to the upper valley. Below the cleft, the trail steepens and finally becomes a scramble ending in a short overhang. A steel chain, firmly anchored in rock, hangs down the trail. By using the chain and natural footholds, you can scramble over the overhang with *relative* ease; but remember that descending is much more difficult. Some hikers may want to turn around rather than tackle the chain. Above the cliff, the trail is easier as it climbs across rocky meadows which turn into scree. Then the trail steepens again until it reaches the hut, elevation 3030 meters, and about 9 km and 5½ hours' hiking time from Bourg St. Pierre.

In winter, these strategically well situated huts are section stops for the high traverse on skis from Chamonix, France to Zermatt, Switzerland. The views from their balconies and the surrounding cliffs are some of the finest in the Alps.

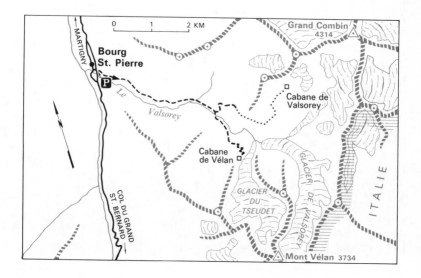

21 LACS DE TSOFERAY

Round trip 16 km, 10 miles
Hiking time 3½ hours up, 3 hours down
High point 2573 meters, 8439 feet
Elevation gain 673 meters, 2207 feet
Map Arolla 283

For variety, this hike has few equals: a huge dam, tunnels to walk through, breathtaking views of Lake Mauvoisin—a fjord-like reservoir—hanging glaciers, the magnificent summit of the Grand Combin, several mountain tarns and, in season, acres of wildflowers.

From Sembrancher on the Grand St. Bernard highway, take the Post Bus or drive 25 km to Mauvoisin, a tiny village with a hotel. Park a short distance beyond in a parking lot below the towering wall of a dam, elevation 1900 meters.

Lac Mauvoisin

Follow the paved road. Walk across the top of the dam and follow a rough, rarely used service road paralleling the eastern side of the lake. First the road passes through a series of tunnels, including one that goes under a waterfall; at 2 km the road switchbacks up a green hillside, climbing 500 meters, and at 3½ km ends at a water diversion project. In good weather there is no problem following the path; although it is sometimes ill defined, it is well marked with painted stripes on rocks. But this is no place to be on a foggy or stormy day. Also, in a short distance there is a stream crossing that can be hazardous on a very hot day when the snow and glaciers are melting.

The trail climbs an easy grade and at 8 km, elevation 2573 meters, reaches Tsoferay Lakes, three shallow tarns surrounded by green meadows. All three provide different views of the majestic Grand Combin. For still another view, climb the green hill to the east overlooking the largest lake. From there you look out at the 5-km-long Breney Glacier.

Experienced hikers can continue for 2 km to the Cabane de Chanrion, elevation 2460 meters, a luxurious mountain hut where meals are served and lodging can be arranged. On the trail past the Tsoferay Lakes you soon descend across a very loose and steep scree slope for about 1 km. From there to the cabin, however, it is easy going. From the cabin, you can take a trail and service road around the west side of the reservoir, making a loop trip of about 20 km.

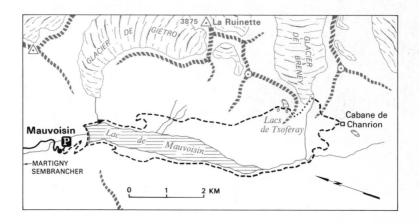

Ladder on Pas de Chevres

22 AROLLA — THE LADDER TRAIL

Round trip 10 km, 6 miles
Hiking time to Cabane des Dix 4 hours
High point 2928 meters, 9604 feet
Elevation gain 1000 meters, 3280 feet in,
**   155 meters, 508 feet out**
Map Arolla 283

If you look out the left side of the Post Bus or your car on the ride up the Val d'Herens from Sion by the upper village road, you will notice tall spires of earth and rock, each with a large stone on top. These sandstone spires were formed through centuries of erosion. The crowning stone protects them from deteriorating completely.

This is just one curiosity of the narrow twisting way up to Arolla. High above the town is a pass, Pas de Chevres, where a long metal ladder has been fixed to the rock walls to permit springtime touring skiers and summer hikers to reach the floor of the Cheilon Glacier and the rustic Cabane des Dix.

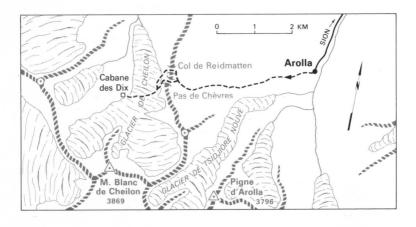

Old farm buildings above Arolla

The correct hiking trail from Arolla is not easy to find. Bear in mind that you must head uphill in a westerly direction. No matter which path you are on, the views are magnificent. To the south is Mont Colon, higher up are the rugged eastern peaks, and on a clear day you can see the tip of the Matterhorn. The trail parallels the Tsidjiore Nouve Glacier for a time and at 3½ km it enters a small basin. Ahead of you is the Pas de Chevre, elevation 2855 meters, where the trail divides. If you have no fear of ladders, keep to the left and plunge down the rungs. If ladders are a problem, go off to the right, through the Col de Reidmatten, and onto the glacier.

From the bottom of the ladder, follow the faint path marked by painted stripes on rock outcroppings to the edge of the Glacier de Cheilon, elevation 2700 meters. At this point, the glacier is fairly flat, with virtually no crevasses. There may be some deep wells cut in the ice by melt water, but unless the glacier is covered with snow, these wells can easily be seen and avoided. If the ice is snow-covered, stay on the well used tracks.

Once across the glacier, climb to the Cabane des Dix, which is located on a knoll surrounded by glaciers, a mere dot on the landscape staring defiantly at the massive Mont Blanc de Cheilon. For the return to Arolla, retrace your steps.

23 MEIDPASS

Round trip 14 km, 9 miles
Hiking time 3 hours up, 2½ down
High point 2790 meters, 9151 feet
Elevation gain 1135 meters, 3723 feet
Map Montana 273

Walk along the Plan Torgnon, a grass plateau with flowers, boulders, small lakes, and on to Meidpass for its mountain views. The hike, reached from the Rhone Valley city of Sierre, starts in the Val d'Anniviers at either the village of Ayer or St. Luc. If starting from Ayer, elevation 1476 meters, one can spend the night at the Hotel Weisshorn located on a 2337-meter-high promontory with a commanding view of mountains and valleys. However, we preferred the route from St. Luc, elevation 1653 meters, as there is a distance and elevation advantage. The two trails from the village have poorly marked trailheads. The easier one leaves from Le Prilet restaurant; but the trail has been almost erased by a wide ski slope which in summer is so depressing that we chose the other route.

Walk the main street toward the church, but just before reaching it, turn left on a narrow road by a small park. Follow this road toward the bottom terminal of a T-bar lift. In a short distance, find a wide path (between two buildings) which climbs steeply. The trail passes a number of chalets, goes beneath the lift, crosses a road, and then enters a forest. There are numerous junctions, but once outside the village the trail is well marked with signs pointing to Meidpass or its abbreviation, "MP." The trail climbs 300 meters and then follows a farm road contouring the mountainside. Near a farmhouse at approximately 3½ km the road intersects the trail; there are several directional signs here so there should be no problem finding the way.

From the farm, follow the trail signed "Meidpass" and "Lac de Combavert." The trees are left behind as the trail climbs another kilometer through pastures and then enters the wide expanse of Plan Torgnon, a flat, rocky plateau with tundra-like vegetation. Although the trail is marked with painted stripes, it can be difficult to follow and impossible in foggy weather. However, in clear weather, the pass is easy to identify just north of a

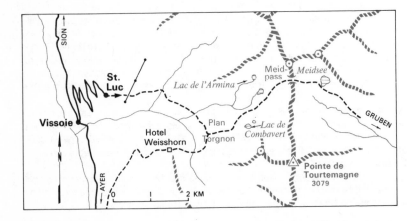

Lac de Combavert

ridge of jagged peaks. Lac de Combavert is a short distance off the trail and its location is well indicated. Many other lakes are visible from the trail.

Below the pass, the way steepens and the top is reached at 7 km, elevation 2790 meters. The pass is the dividing line between French- and German-speaking Switzerland. We recommend hiking another 1½ km to the Meidsee, where there is a fine view of the Weisshorn, a commanding mountain.

Tsidjiore Nouve Glacier

24 LA HAUTE ROUTE

One way 180 km, about 110 miles
Hiking time 10-14 days
High point 3164 meters, 10,378 feet
Elevation gain 10,640 meters, 34,899 feet (cumulative)
Maps Massifs du Mont Blanc 1, Martigny 282, Arolla 283, Montana 273, Visp 274,
** and Mischabel 284**

The high traverse from Chamonix, France to Zermatt, Switzerland is a favorite trip of ski tourers in the winter and spring. There is also, however, a special summer high route for hikers, running through the Alps of two countries with a bit of Italy thrown in. Some

64

people claim that the summer high route—which crosses several passes higher than 2600 meters, takes one through fields of flowers, goes by old farms and lakes, and has splendid views—is at least as beautiful as the classic winter version.

Some sections of the high route are included as day hikes in this book. Other sections go into new territory, some paralleling roads, train tracks, and cable cars. Many hikers do the entire 180 km on foot; while others take short cuts, catching a train or cable car to eliminate less interesting road walks or to gain altitude quickly. Whichever you choose, keep in mind that on a trip in the Alps which extends over several days, there is bound to be some bad weather—rain, wind, snow (even in the month of August)—and good equipment is essential.

The following itinerary lists the trip in day stages. But because of the route's proximity to towns, ski areas, and hotels, you can break up the voyage as you see fit.

1—Chamonix-Les Praz-Lac Blanc (Hike No. 15)-Col des Montets-Col de Balme (Switzerland)-Trient, 26 km, 7 hours

2—Trient-Fenetre d'Arpette, 2665 meters-Champex-Orsieres-Verbier partly by bus or taxi, 35 km, 6-15 hours (or 13 km by trail and 22 km by road)

3—Verbier-Col de Louvie, 2921 meters-Glacier Grand Desert-Col de Prafleurie-Cabane de Prafleurie, 19 km, 9 hours

4—Cabane de Prafleurie-Lac des Dix-Cabane des Dix, 9 km, 4 hours

5—Cabane des Dix-Pas de Chevres (Hike No. 22)-Arolla-Les Hauderes, 21 km, 9 hours

6—Les Hauderes-Col de Torrent, 2918 meters-Lac de Moiry-Grimentz, 18½ km, 8 hours

7—Grimentz-Ayer-Hotel Weisshorn-Meidpass (Hike No. 23), 2790 meters-Gruben, 15 km, 6½ hours

8—Gruben-Augstbordpass, 2894 meters-St. Niklaus-Tasch-Zermatt, 37 km, 7-16 hours, (or 16 km by trail and 20 km by train)

Detailed descriptions of many of these sections can be found in William Reifsnyder's book, **Foot-loose in the Swiss Alps**, Sierra Club, 1974.

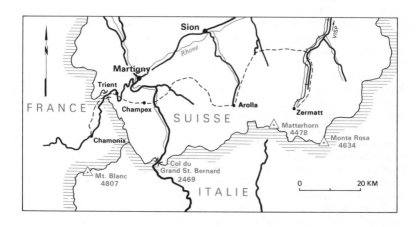

25 AUF KRINDELN
Lotschental Valley

Round trip 8 km, 5 miles
Hiking time 1½ hours up, 1 hour down
High point 2250 meters, 7380 feet
Elevation gain 470 meters, 1542 feet
Map Jungfrau 264

The Lotschental Valley is one of Switzerland's most magnificent—a glacier-carved valley walled in by high ridges and peaks. On the south side are numerous hanging glaciers, on the north side are tantalizing glimpses of a large icefield, and at the head of the valley is Lang Glacier. The valley is so hemmed in that all the hiking trails are short. A trail from the road's end goes for only 4 km to the Lang Glacier's snout; another climbs 1000 meters to the Bietschorn Hut; and several trails follow rushing tributary streams. But the only trail of any length is a 9-km traverse of the valley floor. It stays on the opposite side of the river from the road, and when the road switches sides, so does the trail.

All of these hikes are feasible; we chose the hike up to the steep meadow called Auf Krindeln. Views are superb up and down the Lotschental Valley and across to the knife-like ridge of the Bietschorn. For the most part, the trail is dry and on a sunny day you can get very thirsty. Carry water with you.

In the Rhone Valley, between the cities of Sion and Visp, take the road marked "Goppenstein" with a sign showing an auto train. Follow the road to its end at a huge parking lot accommodating at least 300 cars, elevation 1780 meters. A parking fee is charged. From the lot walk back down the road a short distance, cross a bridge, turn right on the first paved road, and in 300 meters turn right again to a small pond and the start of the trail signed "Krindeln 2½ std." The trail heads right, climbing through the woods in a series of long easy switchbacks, which gradually get shorter and a bit steeper. At 4 km, elevation 2250 meters, you reach the crest of a prominent knoll where there is an array of avalanche control devices and a magnificent view of valley and mountains. The views are not any better above here, but one can wander higher on the steep meadows. We tried to explore the rocky ridge above, but found it difficult.

Bietschorn near Auf Krindeln

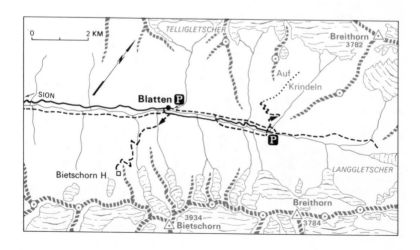

26 TASCHHUTTE

Round trip 14 km, 9 miles
Hiking time 4½ hours up, 3½ hours down
High point 2708 meters, 8883 feet
Elevation gain 1260 meters, 4133 feet
Map Mischabel 284

Almost everything you could imagine finding in the Swiss Alps can be found in this climb to the Taschhutte (hut): active farms, a quaint church, flower-covered meadows, large patches of edelweiss, stunning mountain views, and a herd of chamois!

Taschhutte

From the Rhone Valley city of Visp, catch the train or drive toward Zermatt past lush vineyards and orchards. Debark at Tasch. Since automobile traffic is restricted in Zermatt, hundreds of cars will be parked in the big lot. If you have a car or can afford a taxi, you can save about 4 km and 2½ hours of the hike by driving up an old farm road to the church at Tasch Alps and climbing to the hut from there.

However, since walking is our aim and pleasure, this hike is described from the Tasch train station, elevation 1438 meters. Go up the street, take the only right, and walk towards Zermatt for a short distance, then turn left onto a paved road, following the signs marked "Taschalps." This road takes you to a cluster of buildings at the edge of the valley floor. Find the trailhead between two old barns. The trail climbs steeply through a forest. Between the trees are views of the mountains and a distant glimpse of the Matterhorn. The trail crosses the old farm road several times before reaching Tasch Alps (elevation 2203 meters) and its small church surrounded by pastureland. Although the farm road continues up the valley, this is not the route to the Tasch hut. Instead, climb up a rough service road used by farm tractors which supply the hut. On the road, the Matterhorn has disappeared from view, but the Weisshorn and its many glaciers loom larger the higher you climb. After climbing for 3 steep km, you reach the 2708-meter-high Taschhutte, where there are approximately 40 bunks and hot food. The hut may well be crowded since it is the starting point for hikes to the glaciers and climbs of many high peaks east of Zermatt.

More than fifty chamois live near the hut and can easily be seen, particularly in early morning. You will also find plenty of edelweiss, a sturdy plant able to withstand almost any weather conditions. However, it must not be picked.

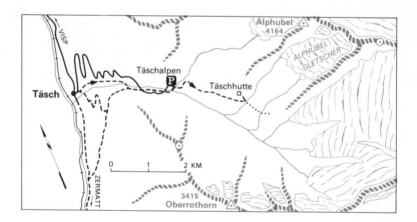

Matterhorn from trail to Schonbielhutte

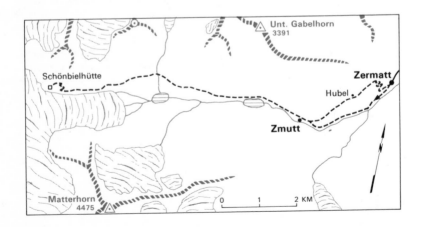

27 SCHONBIELHUTTE

Round trip 22 km, 14 miles
Hiking time 4 hours up, 3½ down
High point 2694 meters, 8836 feet
Elevation gain 1089 meters, 3572 feet
Map Arolla 283, Mischabel 284

Old farm buildings at Hubel

By being the first person to scale the Matterhorn in 1865, Edward Whymper did a great deal to make this peak the most famous in the Alps. The Matterhorn can be seen from many vantage points: from Zermatt itself, from the Italian side (where it is called the Cervino), or from faraway summits like the Pigne d'Arolla and Mont Blanc. One of our favorite views, however, is seen on the way up to the Schonbielhutte via the tiny village of Zmutt, 3 km outside of Zermatt. The trail to the hut passes so close to the base of the Matterhorn that one can barely see the summit. And yet that towering pinnacle seems to dominate everything.

This hike can be a long day's outing or, better still, include an overnight stay. From the Zermatt railroad station, elevation 1605 meters, walk along the main street, and just beyond the last road junction find directional signs indicating "Zmutt." The trail climbs through fields and woods to a small cluster of weathered farm buildings surrounding a miniature church. The trail continues out of Zmutt, past a small reservoir across from a complex of water conduits and reservoirs so familiar in the Swiss Alps, where just about all the rivers under glaciers have been tapped for hydroelectric power. Giving glimpses of the tortured Tiefmatten Glacier, the trail dips under a cliff, then up again onto a lateral moraine opposite the snout of the Z'mutt Glacier. Views have expanded dramatically, and one can discern the sharp ridges of the Dent d'Herens, the Dent Blanche, and the towering Matterhorn rising up into the sky.

For about 4 km, the trail climbs gradually, passing under a glacier which literally hangs on the side of the Pte. de Zinal. Then the trail switchbacks up and reaches the Schonbielhutte at 2694 meters, 11 km from Zermatt. The hut is located on a knoll surrounded by glaciers, with a superb panorama of mountains.

To vary the return trip, leave the main trail at Zmutt. Follow a trail to the left which climbs steeply at first and then traverses to Hubel, a cluster of farm buildings, before its steep descent to Zermatt.

28 GORNERGRAT

One way 12 km, 7½ miles
Hiking time 4 hours
High point 3090 meters, 10,135 feet
Elevation loss 1500 meters, 4920 feet
Map Mischabel 284

Like all beautiful mountains, the Matterhorn and Monte Rosa can be seen in many ways from many angles: soaring above an alpine village; with green meadows and colorful flowers in the foreground; reflected in streams, or casting their shadows on high glaciers. This day hike takes you to a major viewpoint.

You can get to the heights quickly by taking the cog railway from the Zermatt station to the Gornergrat at 3090 meters. Or you can walk up and down. The latter trip means almost 24 km of mountain scrambling, and for a day hike that's a lot. So we decided to take the cog railway up and, after a good hearty picnic, while away the afternoon coming down through the forests and meadows overlooking Zermatt.

The cog railway ride is one of the most extraordinary in the world. As you inch up the mountain, the foliage changes, snow comes closer, the seracs and crevasses of the glaciers loom above—it's a cold, eerie world. From the Gornergrat you can even take a cable car over snowfields and glaciers up to the Stockhorn. However, climbing down from there can be tricky, and sometimes mountaineering skills and equipment are necessary. So for most hikers, the Gornergrat is high enough.

The downhill trail starts on the Monte Rosa side of the railroad tracks. It descends steeply through arctic tundra-type vegetation, past a small tarn, then past breathtaking views of the massive Gorner Glacier, which flows from Monte Rosa and the Breithorn. Near the Rifelberg Hotel, the trail enters the forest. At the junction, be sure to take the right-hand trail, which follows the mountain contours for another kilometer to the alpine village of Findeln. The barns and farmhouses clustered around a small church are used by farmers during the summer months.

From here you can catch a chair lift down to Zermatt, or continue hiking through the trees until you arrive at pastureland a short distance above the village. There in front of you is the classic view of the Matterhorn.

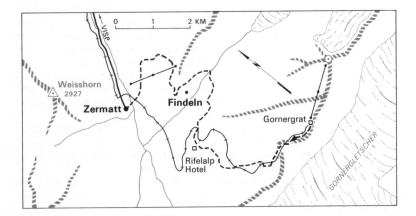

Matterhorn from trail near Rifelberg Hotel

29 GROSSER ALETSCH GLACIER

One way 14 km, 9 miles
Hiking time 4 hours
High point 2893 meters, 9489 feet
Elevation gain 200 meters, 656 feet
Elevation loss 1180 meters, 3870 feet
Map Jungfrau 264

The Aletsch is the longest glacier in the Alps. Chamois, lush mountain views, and the deep green meadows of the Bettmeralp can be seen between the cable cars and chair lifts. Unfortunately, there are no long trails left, but the views are still there. With its many hotels and huts, this area is a good place to spend a night or two, watch sunrises and sunsets, and observe the animals. To do and see all of this, you can use the cable cars and railroad to advantage: you exchange solitude for quantity. These mechanical devices greatly facilitate loop trips.

From the Rhone Valley city of Brig, drive or take the train to Fiesch and ride the cable car to a 2893-meter shoulder of the Eggishorn. From here the views are fantastic and on clear days you can pick out the Matterhorn. The Grosser Aletsch Glacier, 26 km long, flowing from the Jungfrau, makes a wide turn below the Eggishorn. The hike starts from here; be sure to ask if there is ice and snow on the trail. If there is, don't take a chance. Return on the cable car to the middle terminal.

From the upper terminal, follow the ridge a short distance to the north, then take a steep trail switchbacking down a rocky hillside until you reach a service road and hotel. The service road takes you west, back to the middle terminal of the cable car, for a hike of approximately 4 km. From here follow the ups and downs of the service road to the 1948-meter-high village of Donnerstafel at 8 km. Either go all the way to Donnerstafel and climb back up to the shallow lake of Bettmersee, or find a trail to the right crossing under a chair lift. Continue on to Blausee, a smaller lake surrounded by green meadows, views, and lots of people.

Grosser Aletsch Glacier near Blausee

Blausee

From Blausee, follow the trail which climbs over a rocky ridge at an elevation of 2250 meters. Cross the ridge for views of the big glacier once again. For the best views, detour upward on any trail that follows the ridgeline or along the hillside. For closeup views of the ice, there is a trail to the edge of the glacier. If you are there early in the morning or at dusk you may see a chamois or two. A herd of them lives on the upper ridge.

To return, follow any trail headed down from the ridgetop toward Rieder Furka, then catch the cable car at Riederalp, 14 km, elevation 1909 meters, to Morel, where you can take a train back to Fiesch.

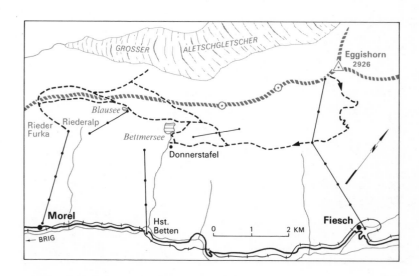

Fishing in Oeschinensee

30 OESCHINENSEE

Round trip to Unter Bergli 10 km, 6 miles
Hiking time 4 hours
High point 1767 meters, 5796 feet
Elevation gain 420 meters, 1378 feet
Map Wildstrubel 264, Jungfrau 264

Almost every Swiss calendar contains a picture of Oeschinensee Lake. Since it is a lovely spot to hike to, we decided to try and duplicate the picture. We found that the best time to shoot it is late afternoon when the light angles onto the lake and the shadows provide contrast. The lake trail is so short and crowded it is best once you have savored the view, to hike on to the Gasthaus Unter Bergli, a small hotel where views are more grandiose and there are fewer people. More experienced hikers may want to continue farther to the Blumlisalphutte.

The hike starts in the city of Kandersteg, reached by train or road from the cities of Bern and Thun. The trail is well signed both from the railroad station and the highway. You can ride a chair lift, thus eliminating all climbing to the lake. But this is the popular thing to do, so there are often long waiting lines; it is best to use your legs.

Hike the steep jeep road starting at Oeschinensee stream near the chair lift at 1200 meters. The left-side trail crosses a bridge to the right bank, passes below a waterfall, crosses the stream again, and climbs steeply up to the lakeshore at 3 km, elevation 1578 meters. Before going on, hike the lakeshore. The scenery is even better than what the calendar pictures show. When you have seen enough or want a change, go back toward the restaurants at the outlet of the lake and find the trail signed "Gasthaus Unter Bergli," which climbs a ledge on the north side of the lake to the Gasthaus at 5 km, elevation 1767 meters.

From here on the trail becomes quite difficult and requires some concentration. As always, the problem is not the uphill sections where you can easily see where your feet go, but the steep downhills over uneven ground. Those who are capable will find the hike to Blumlisalphutte, 4 km farther and 1344 meters higher, well worth the effort.

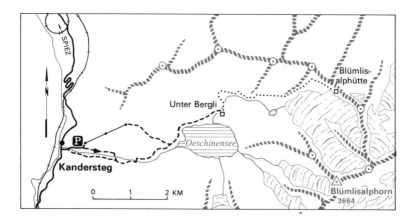

Lauterbrunnen Valley

31 WENGEN

One way 12 km, 7½ miles
Hiking time 3 hours
High point 2229 meters, 7311 feet
Elevation gain 200 meters, 656 feet
Elevation loss 1434 meters, 4704 feet
Map Interlaken 254

Ride a cog railroad to the base of the Eiger, walk an easy trail along a green ridge with views of Grindelwald and the Wetterhorn, and then drop down to Wengen and see Lauterbrunnen Valley, a textbook example of a U-shaped glacier-carved valley. We have returned many times to do this hike because it is one of our favorites in Switzerland.

From Interlaken, go by train or car to the town of Lauterbrunnen and take the cog railroad to Kleine Scheidegg, elevation 2061 meters. From Kleine Scheidegg you can see the famous north face of the Eiger. If any climbers are on the face, and often there are, their progress can be followed by telescope. From Kleine Scheidegg the railroad tunnels up inside the Eiger to a station near the top of the Jungfrau, where there is a

Queen of the cow herd returning from summer pasture

superb viewpoint. Even though there is no place to hike from there and the train trip is expensive, it is well worth every Swiss franc.

Back down at the Kleine Scheidegg station, head north along a prominent ridge with views of Grindelwald, farms, and mountains. At 4 km you reach a hotel at 2229 meters, the high point of this hike. From there the trail drops over the west side of the ridge, crosses under the wires of a cable car, and descends, at times very steeply, towards the alpine town of Wengen and views into the Lauterbrunnen Valley. As the trail levels out and approaches the farmlands above Wengen, there are many branching paths and service roads. The way is well marked and the distance to the town is about 8 km.

For best views of the Lauterbrunnen Valley, detour on any likely looking right-hand trail where a broad shoulder gives a straight look up the valley. The shoulder ends as a cliff, so when you are satisfied with the view head back to Wengen. At the Wengen railroad station, find the trail down to Lauterbrunnen, 12 km from Kleine Scheidegg.

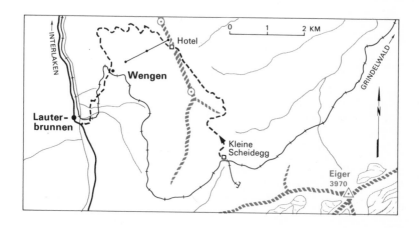

32 OBERHORNSEE

Round trip 16 km, 10 miles
Hiking time 4 hours up, 3 hours down
High point 2065 meters, 6773 feet
Elevation gain 1155 meters, 3788 feet
Map Jungfrau 264

This is one of the most rewarding hikes in the Interlaken area. There are no service roads, cable cars, waterworks, or manicured ski slopes to mar the views. The farms and mountain hotels are still on the simple side, and man's presence has left few permanent scars. On the way up to this lake you hike through a cool forest and green meadows where the chamois graze, past rushing torrents and waterfalls.

Chamois at Obersteinberg

Although this is a fine jaunt in cloudy weather when the colors are subtle, the chamois less timid, and the people fewer, the hike becomes sensational when the weather is fine, the mountains are seen against a backdrop of clear blue sky, and the glacier-covered summits of the Jungfrau and Breithorn and the bare cliffs of the Ellstabhorn are all visible.

From Interlaken, by bus or auto follow the Lauterbrunnen Valley to the parking lot at road's end in the small village of Stechelberg, elevation 910 meters. The trail, wide enough for a tractor, starts up the left (east) side of the valley. At ¾ km, it crosses the Weisse Lutschine River and then heads steeply up the right side of the valley. At 2 km, the trail passes a small hotel at Trachsel-lauenen, the end of the tractor route. At 2½ km the trail forks. Both routes go to the same place and are equally rewarding. The left fork follows the torrent, then forks again with a possible side trip to a large waterfall. The right fork is in better condition and offers fine views.

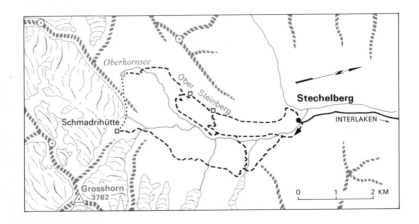

Oberhornsee

The right-fork trail switchbacks steeply up to alpine meadows which offer views of the valley and mountains. At 4½ km, elevation 1685 meters, you reach a hotel at Obersteinberg, then contour to a second hotel at 5 km, both hotels have remarkable views. Once again the trail pretty much follows the contours of the meadows, with a few ups and downs, until it crosses a stream. Then it steepens and switchbacks up a rocky pomontory a short distance from the Oberhornsee, a small lake at 8 im, elevation 2065 meters. Views are breathtaking.

The best times to see chamois are in the early morning or evening or on a rainy day. Look for them on the edges of meadows above the hotels at Obersteinberg and on the rocky meadows near the lake. To vary your descent, hike past the two hotels and stay high up to catch the trail marked "Murren." Follow this route down the valley until you are directly above the village of Stechelberg. Find a trail which switchbacks steeply down to the starting point. Or, for even greater variety, from Oberhornsee follow a paint marked trail east to the Schmadri Hutte, elevation 2263 meters, and return on the opposite side of the valley.

33 FAULHORN

One way 15 km, 9½ miles
Hiking time 6 hours
High point 2600 meters, 8528 feet
Elevation gain 700 meters, 2296 feet
Map Interlaken 254

The first time we attempted this hike we were engulfed in clouds most of the way and were tantalized by fleeting glimpses of the beautiful sights. So we hiked it again on a clear day. The hike follows a high ridge with the low hills of northern Switzerland on one side and, on the south side, the frightening north face of the Eiger and the glacier-clad mountains of the Bernese Oberland. As you walk along the ridge, you can look down over 2000 meters and see sailboats on the Brienzer See, and, in the valley on the south side, tiny villages snuggled beneath the hills. These views are so dramatic that you should attempt the hike only on a clear day. Though main and side trails are well marked, the route crosses some chutes, and snow may still be present even in August.

By using uphill transportation, you can make this a round trip. From Interlaken travel to Wilderswil, and from there take the cog railroad to Schynige Platte, elevation 2067 meters. At the railroad station, find the trail marked "Faulhorn." It contours slightly up on the south side of the ridge. At just over 2 km, you reach a high point; then a gentle slope downward brings you to a short series of switchbacks leading up to a 2067-meter-high pass at 4 km. Now the way climbs gently as it contours a hillside high above the Sagistalsee, a small lake with two farms on its shores. Then the trail turns a corner and passes Weberhutte, a small restaurant. Beyond the restaurant, the trail steepens slightly, climbing a barren ridge, and at 9 km, elevation 2660 meters, it goes a few meters below a large hotel on top of a promontory called the Faulhorn. From here you will have the best view down to Brienzer See to the north and the Jungfrau Range to the south.

From the hotel the trail then descends to the Bachsee, two beautiful lakes surrounded by green hills. From the lakes, either take a lower trail marked "Grindelwald," losing

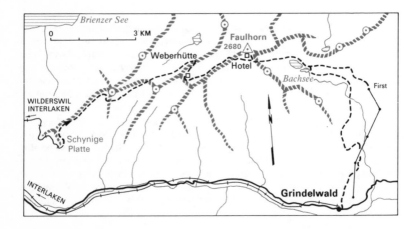

Cow grazing near Bachsee

some 1200 meters (a healthy drop and a good 2-hour walk), or from Bachsee remain on the upper trail, which takes you to the top terminal of the First chair lift at 15 km. Then ride the lift down in comfort to Grindelwald and take the train back to the starting point.

34 GROSSE SCHEIDEGG

One way 15 km, 9½ miles
Hiking time 1½ hours to pass, 2½ down
High point 3000 meters, 9840 feet
Elevation gain 100 meters, 328 feet
Elevation loss 905 meters, 2968 feet
Map Interlaken 254

Hike to a mountain pass and tiny Hornseeli Lake under the towering north side of the Wetterhorn, the beautiful mountain that dominates the resort city of Grindelwald. This high mountain scenery is equalled only in hikes around Chamonix, Zermatt, or Austria's Grossglockner.

Many high-altitude farms are found along the trail, and civilization has left its impression here in other ways. While private automobiles are barred, the trip can be made entirely by motorbus; or most of the elevation can be gained by use of the chair lift. Of course, it is possible to walk both ways. There is much to see and many branching roads and trails, so that it is possible to return by a different route. However, for a day hike, the pass offers the major interest. So with some chagrin we rode the chair lift up, hiked around, and walked back down.

From Interlaken, take the road or train to Grindelwald, elevation 1057 meters. In the center of town find the First chair lift. There are several sections to the lift, but just remain on it until it reaches the top station at an elevation of 2167 meters. From there take the trail headed east (right). With considerable ups and downs, walk along the hillside to Oberlager, a small cluster of farm buildings. Continue on and at 3½ km you reach a fork. The right trail follows the divide down and at 5 km arrives at Grosse Scheidegg; but for the time being, stay on the left trail and hike to the second farmhouse cluster called Oberlager.

To reach Hornseeli Lake above, go beyond Oberlager, cross the stream, and soon you reach a junction. Stay on the left trail for a short distance, and then leave it and make your way uphill to right on a well trod path that climbs steeply to the lake.

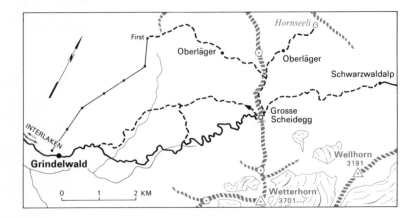

Hornseeli Lake and cloud-covered Wetterhorn

To return, retrace your steps to the intersection with the main trail going down to the pass and hotel-restaurant at Grosse Scheidegg. From there, either follow the paved road 10 km back to Grindelwald, or follow the trail that can be seen going down a green ridge. The trail is a lot steeper than the road, but easily saves a kilometer of relatively uninteresting hiking. If there is no reason to return to Grindelwald, an alternative is to follow the service road eastward from Grosse Scheidegg down to Schwarzwaldalp and eventually back to Interlaken by bus. In this case, it would be wise to check bus schedules in advance at Grindelwald.

35 ALBERT HEIM HUTTE

Loop trip 6 km, 3¾ miles
Hiking time 1 hour first half, 2 hours second half
High point 2541 meters, 8334 feet
Elevation gain 520 meters, 1706 feet
Map Sustenpass 255

On this hike, you walk around a steep ridge with views of glacier-clad Galenstock and the exciting rock spires of Winterstock. The trail traverses high above the mountain village of Realp; from there you can see the complex system of avalanche fences that protect the village 1000 meters below.

From Andermatt, drive or take the Post Bus to the tiny village of Tiefenbach, located high on a steep mountain slope on the east side of Furka Pass. From the village,follow the highway 200 meters toward the pass and find a dirt road leading uphill, elevation 2180 meters. It is possible to drive the road 1 km to a new trailhead or take the old trail. The distance is about the same, but there is a saving of 200 meters' climbing on the new trail, which is well marked. However, we enjoyed hiking the old trail. Follow the dirt road 100 meters and at the first switchback look for a trail headed toward a stream to the left and marked with red paint. The way is very rough, but the flowers are plentiful. At about 1½ km the new trail joins the old. At 2 km you reach the hut, elevation 2541 meters.

From the hut, you can make a very pleasant side trip by following a path south along the ridgetop to a 2591-meter vantage point.

For the loop trip, return to the hut, backtrack down the trail a short distance, and follow a climbers' path towards the glacier, paralleling a pipeline. Look for a faint trail marked with red and white paint. Cross a rockslide and pass under the north side of the hut, dropping steeply down a gully towards the east. Although the trail through the rocks is faint, it can be seen on the green hillside beyond. In 1 km, the trail levels off somewhat and crosses three streams. These crossings are not bridged and they could cause problems when the water is high. This trail eventually descends all the way to the valley floor, so be careful to stay on the upper path. It would be best to refer to the topographical map. After the third stream crossing, follow an unmarked trail that climbs slightly,

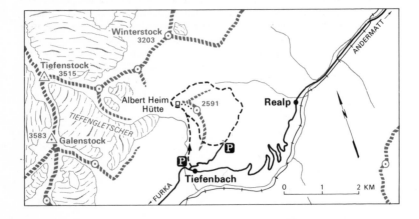

Albert Heim Hutte and Winterstock (mountain)

then contours for ½ km to intersect a bulldozed construction road. Follow the bulldozer track up for 100 meters, passing some massive avalanche control fences. The track levels off and becomes a usable road. At 5 km, pass the new trailhead to the Albert Heim Hutte and then descend to the starting point at the village of Tiefenbach.

87

36 CHELENALP HUTTE

Round trip 14 km, 9 miles
Hiking time 3½ hours in, 3 hours out
High point 2350 meters, 7708 feet
Elevation gain 687 meters, 2253 feet in, 150 meters, 492 feet out
Map Sustenpass 255 or Urseren 1231

This hike provides three different choices: the first is 2½ km from the start, the Bergsee Hutte located next to an alpine tarn with sweeping views. It's an easy, rewarding jaunt. Second is the Damma Hutte, located on the other side of the Chelen Valley, 3 hours away. Third is the far more interesting climb to the Chelenalp Hutte.

From the town of Goschenen, north of Andermatt, drive or ride the Post Bus 10 km to Goscheneralp. Park in the lot near a huge earth dam behind which is the Goscheneralpsee. The trail begins at the upper end of the parking lot, climbs in a series of short switchbacks to two small tarns, levels off, and in 1 km reaches a junction with the trail to the Bergsee Hutte. Keep left and descend first gently and then steeply to the head of a reservoir, losing virtually all the elevation you gained. At 2½ km, at the edge of the torrent called Chelenreuss, the trail forks. The left fork crosses the torrent and climbs steeply to the Damma Hutte, elevation 2438 meters. For the Chelenalp Hutte, stay on the right side of the stream. In places it dashes over rocks; elsewhere it meanders lazily along the valley, which has a classic U-shape formed by ancient glaciers; the valley floor is covered with flowers.

At about 6½ km, near the rubble-covered snout of the Chelen Glacier, the trail leaves the valley floor and climbs steeply 200 meters to the Chelenalp Hutte. From the hut's balcony you have splendid views of glaciers, alpine pastures, roaring torrents, and the now distant reservoir.

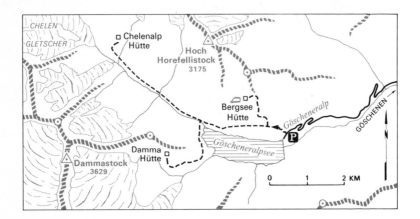

Chelenreuss (river)

37 GEMSFAIREN (KLAUSENPASS)

Round trip 4 km, 2½ miles
Hiking time 2 hours
High point 1951 meters, 6401 feet
Elevation gain 261 meters, 856 feet
Map Klausenpass 246

An easy hike on a farm road takes you to Gemsfairen, a high pasture with views of peaks and a deep, U-shaped valley.

From Klausenpass drive east 4½ km to a flat meadow under a 200-meter-high headwall. Park near the farm road, elevation 1690 meters, that crosses the meadow and switchbacks up the opposite side of the valley. The trail starts on a service road and is marked "Gemsfairen 1 std. Chamerstock 4 std., und Clariden Hutte." It is well graded and ideal for leisurely walking. It makes a short switchback, passes through a tunnel, and climbs. The views improve with each step; the road traverses above the dramatic valley that once must have contained a mighty glacier and now houses the Fatschbach River. At 4 km, elevation 1951 meters, the road passes a farmhouse, and a few meters farther ends abruptly at the edge of a huge fan-shaped meadow with several streams of crystal-clear water.

Here one can relax and marvel at the ridges leading west under 3267-meter-high Mount Clariden, a peak with numerous small glaciers. If you are energetic, go east following the trail to the Clariden Hutte, 2453 meters, another 18 km for the round trip. We decided to relax and had lunch beside one of the clear streams; then we walked west over rocky knolls and green ridges until we reached the edge of a huge talus slope and turned back.

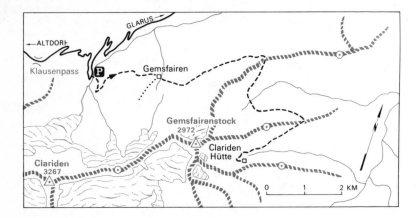

Service road to Gemsfairen

38 ALTEINSEE (AROSA)

Round trip 8 km, 5 miles
Hiking time 4½ hours
High point 2251 meters, 7383 feet
Elevation gain 640 meters, 2099 feet
Map Bergen 258 and Prattigau 248

This steep, occasionally rough trail starts along a wooded river bank, then climbs past a beautiful waterfall to meadows, views, more waterfalls, and a shallow lake.

The trail begins on the outskirts of the resort town of Arosa; but locating the trailhead is difficult. If you arrive by car, turn left at an Esso station at the entrance to town. If you arrive by train, walk around either side of Obersee, the lake directly in front of the station. Head away from the main part of town to the Esso station and from there head downhill on Neubachstrasse to Untersee Platz. Keep going until you reach a large waterworks at the end of the road, elevation 1610 meters.

Follow a service road in front of the waterworks. This soon becomes a wide trail which climbs along the Welschtobelbach River. At 1½ km cross a wooden bridge; shortly after, cross Alteinbach stream on another bridge. The trail steepens noticeably and switchbacks up, alternating between a scrub forest and a rock slide. Near the top of the slide is a junction. Since the directional sign is often displaced by avalanches, note that the left fork makes a worthwhile detour to an overlook of the beautiful Altein Waterfall. The right fork switchbacks up a steep terrace, and 3 km farther it reaches open meadows. From here on the trail is badly eroded by cow tracks and at times it is hard to follow. It boulder-hops Altein stream and continues up in sight of two more waterfalls. At 4 km, elevation 2251 meters, it passes a few meters above crescent-shaped Alteinsee (a lake).

The lake is the center of a kilometer-wide meadow with meandering bubbling brooks worthy of Wordsworth. There are ridges to explore and meadows to roam in, and it's a marvelous place to stretch out and relax. From the lake the trail continues another 2 km to Alteiner Pass at 2491 meters, where a sketchy trail leads to the 2764-meter summit of Valbellahorn Mountain, which rises directly behind the lake.

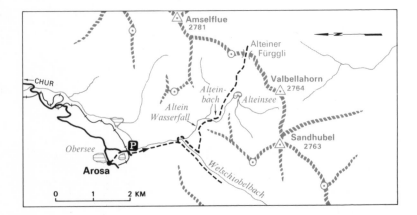

Altein Waterfall

When we made this trip, we lost our way right at the trailhead. Our map predated the waterworks and the trail signs didn't help much; so we ended up on an old logging road behind the waterworks. The road ended and we just bushwhacked through the forest until we found the correct trail. For our efforts we were rewarded with a closeup view of two bucks with beautiful antlers who were as surprised to see us as we were to see them.

39 FUORCLA DA GRIALETSCH

Round trip 8 km, 5 miles
Hiking time 2 hours each way
High point 2537 meters, 8321 feet
Elevation gain 537 meters, 1761 feet
Map Wanderkarte Davos or Bergun 258

This is an ideal family hike or an afternoon jaunt to a small lake, mountain views, and a mountain hut. From early July, you will find acres and acres of alpine rose—rhododendron bushes with red-pink blossoms. Another attraction of this hike is the drive to the trailhead up a narrow road past numerous old farm buildings, a surprising contrast to the cement city of Davos nearby.

From Davos drive a narrow paved road 13 km to the tiny village of Durrboden. The road is too narrow for the Post Bus, so if you have no car you must either hire a taxi or walk an excellent trail that parallels the road. Hiking has its advantages. It provides plenty of time to enjoy the old farm buildings; besides, there are several restaurants, hotels, and cafes along the way should you wish to interrupt the hike.

The road ends at the parking lot at 2007 meters. The trail is very poor and spotted with cobblestones. When it forks, keep left. Unexpectedly, at about the halfway point, the trail becomes well graded and hiking is much easier. At approximately 3½ km the trail passes Furkasee, a shallow tarn, and at 4 km reaches Fuorcla Da Grialetsch, a pass at 2537 meters. Hike a few meters farther to the Grialetsch hut and a commanding view of the Vadret da Grialetsch, a wide glacier.

At the pass the trail divides into three rough tracks to the Fluelapass road; all are marked with red and white paint. The Fluelapass road has frequent Post Bus service, and if you haven't left a car in Durrboden, the bus is an excellent way to get back to Davos. For ramblings around the hut and better views, hike the uppermost of the three trails, to a high shoulder on the side of Piz Radont; or follow a climber's path which rises to a shoulder of Piz Grialetsch and goes across the top of a moraine to the edge of the Grialetsch Glacier.

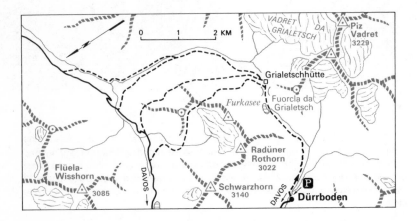

Furkasee

We started this hike around 5:00 a.m. and were the first people to leave the parking lot. We hadn't gone more than 500 meters when two chamois came charging down the mountainside. They crossed the trail about 100 meters ahead of us, made a big loop, crossed 100 meters behind us, and, still running full tilt, disappeared up the mountainside.

95

40 VAL MULIX

Round trip 11 km, 7 miles
Hiking time 4 hours
High point 2622 meters, 8600 feet
Elevation gain 833 meters, 2732 feet
Map Bergun 258

Many trails in the Alps lead to more impressive views but Val Mulix is uncrowded and, at least on the rainy day we were there, it offered a chance to enjoy the solitude of forest, alpine meadows, and a small lake that is frozen much of the year.

The trail starts at the tiny village of Naz. There is one small hotel in the area but no stores or campgrounds. Since the train does not stop at Naz, get off beforehand at the equally small village of Preda, and walk 1 km toward Naz. You may be lucky enough to see a deer with its fawn grazing in a pasture. We did, and it was one of the highlights of the day.

At Naz, follow a short road to the uppermost farm building where the trailhead can be found at 1789 meters. The trail enters the forest, crosses a turbulent stream via a wooden bridge, and climbs up steeply for about 1½ km to a fork. The well worn right trail heads up to Pass d'Ela. Take the lesser used left path which follows the Mulix River up the Val Mulix. The trail levels a bit and at times becomes indistinct as it crosses a marshy alpine pasture; but even if you lose it, the only route is up the valley. About 800 meters from the fork you pass a farm hut, and the trail steepens. At about 4 km, the valley and trail make an abrupt right turn and both end at Lake Negr, elevation 2622 meters, at 5½ km.

Naz is also the starting point for a full-day or overnight hike, much of which is above timberline. Take the same trail to the fork, but instead of going left, follow the steep trail to the right, which switches back and forth through the woods to timberline and a small restaurant. Continue steadily up through green meadows and boulder slopes to the Pass d'Ela at 2725 meters. From there the trail, marked by cairns and painted stripes, descends gradually for another 3 km to the d'Ela hut at 2252 meters. From the hut one can continue down 7 km to either Bergun or Filisur.

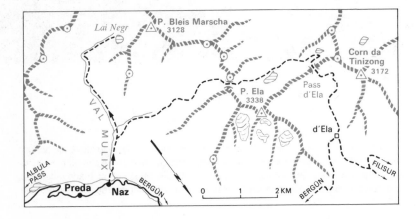

Trail from Naz

Alp Grimmels

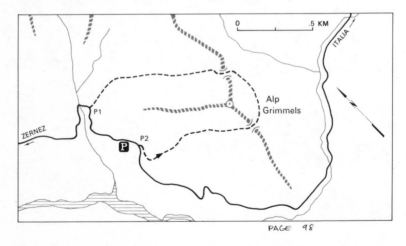

41 ALP GRIMMELS
Swiss National Park

Loop trip 7 km, 4¼ miles
Hiking time 1½ hours to Alp, 2½ hours loop
High point 2100 meters, 6888 feet
Elevation gain 300 meters, 984 feet
Map Ofenpass 259

The main features of this forest hike in the Swiss National Park are the many red deer and marmots that the hiker has a good chance of seeing. It's also a good introduction— to the way the Swiss manage the rich natural resources in the park.

In most countries, national parks are formed to protect some unique feature such as scenery or wildlife. If scenery were the only criterion, all of Switzerland would qualify as a park. In comparison to the rest of the Alps, the mountains in the Swiss National Park are relatively tame. However, the park is a large nature preserve where flowers are not picked by man or eaten by cows, and animals are not hunted. Man is the intruder and must abide by strict rules. Hikers are allowed on park trails, but they must stay on them. A tired hiker may rest alongside the trail, but lunch stops are permitted only at designated locations. No camping is allowed. All of the rules are explained at the Park Visitor Center at Zernez.

From Zernez, travel the Ofenpass road for 9 km to Park Place No. 2, elevation 1800 meters. The unmarked trailhead is on the uphill side of the highway. In ½ km, you reach a junction. Keep straight ahead.

The trail climbs very steeply, gaining 200 meters. It then levels off and traverses a steep mountainside to a wooded pass at 2100 meters. Beyond the pass, the trail descends slightly to Alp Grimmels and a rest area (no water available), elevation 2000 meters, at 2½ km.

At daybreak and dusk the meadow is heavily grazed by red deer. During the heat of day, the deer retreat to the woods, chewing their cuds. However, marmots love heat and are generally visible near rocks and feeding in the meadow. From here continue to a junction in 3¼ km, then keep left and descend a dry valley. At 6 km, you return to the highway at Park Place No. 1 and are only 1 km from your starting point.

Marmot living in Alp Grimmels

42 ALP TRUPCHUN
Swiss National Park

Round trip 12 km, 7½ miles
Hiking time 4 hours
High point 2040 meters, 6691 feet
Elevation gain 380 meters, 1246 feet
Map Wanderkarte Oberengadin-Bernina or Ofenpass 259

Alp Trupchun is part of the Swiss National Park. Flowers and animals are protected and the area is noted for its wildlife—red deer, steinbok (ibex), chamois, and marmots. In May and early June, the animals are frequently seen along the valley bottom trail; but as the snow melts they move higher up, and in summer they are often just tiny dots on a distant mountainside. The trail to the high madows is attraction enough; but the abundant animals and flowers make it very special.

From the town of S-chanf in the Inn Valley, walk or ride on the road marked either "Varusch" or "National Park" 2 km to the road's end, elevation 1660 meters. When we hiked this trail, the first kilometer was being widened to road width, so now it may be possible to drive higher up.

From the road's end, follow a jeep trail ½ km, cross Ova da Varusch (a stream) and you attain the rustic Varusch hut in 1½ km. The jeep road ends at the hut, where there is a confusion of trails. Stay at the stream level; in 1¾ km the trail enters the National Park. Then it follows the stream and climbs steadily. At 3 km the trail crosses the stream and 500 meters farther on recrosses it, then reaches a junction with the Fuorcla Val Sassa trail (Hike No. 43). Keep right. Next, the trail switchbacks up a steep hillside and levels off. Soon trees give way to the lush flower and grass meadows of Alp Trupchun. Well up

Telephoto of ibex in Alp Trupchun

in the meadow is a rest area beside an old farmhouse now used by park rangers.

Early morning and evening, when the animals are feeding, are the best times of day to observe them. During the heat of the day they often lie down and are hard to spot. Herds of 20-50 red deer feed on the open slopes while the steinbok tend to walk the ridgelines. To see the animals better, many hikers bring field glasses and some even carry telescopes and tripods.

Animal viewing is sometimes better higher up toward Trupchun Pass, 2782 meters, overlooking Switzerland and Italy. A park ranger can tell you where you are most likely to see the animals.

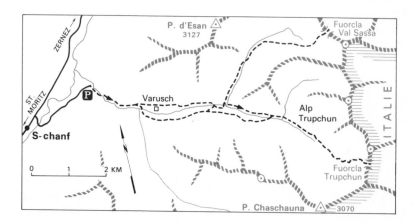

Muschauns stream

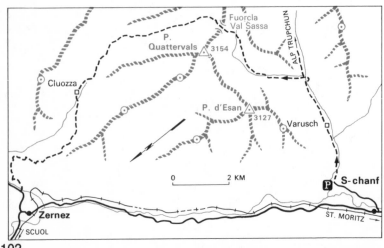

43 FUORCLA VAL SASSA
Swiss National Park

One way 24 km, 15 miles
Hiking time 1½ days
High point 2857 meters, 9731 feet
Elevation gain 1425 meters, 4674 feet
Map Ofenpass 259

The Swiss National Park is the scene of this 1½-day jaunt from S-chanf to Zernez, or vice versa. Since camping is prohibited in the park, the first day's hike is to the Blockhaus (chamanna) Cluozza, a rustic mountain inn where you must sleep; it's a long walk. The trail traverses a high barren pass with a view of the Piz Quattervals, the highest peak in the park.

From S-chanf follow the directions for the Val Trupchun in Hike No. 42. Pass the Varusch hut and enter the park, continuing upstream 3 km to an intersection. The right fork follows Trupchun stream to Val Trupchun. Take the left fork and immediately cross Muschauns stream on a wooden bridge. The trail, rather sketchy at times, crosses the stream again at 4 km and then climbs steeply to another crossing. Finally at 9 km it reaches Fuorcla Val Sassa, a 2857-meter-high pass. On the far side of the pass the route is marked by paint. It goes over scree and snow patches, making it difficult to follow in poor weather. Eventually, the trail enters the forest, and at 15 km from the road's end reaches Blockhaus Cluozza, elevation 1882 meters. This is the only back-country inn in the park.

Next day, continue on the same trail, dropping 80 meters to a stream crossing; then contour and climb 280 meters to a ridge overlooking the Inn Valley. From here the trail descends in a series of switchbacks to farm fields. The trail eventually becomes a farm road, crosses the Spol River, and at 24 km reaches the Ofenpass highway about 1 km from Zernez. Return to S-chanf by train or bus.

Lone chamois feeding in the Muschauns Valley

Tschierva Hutte and Tschierva Glacier

44 TSCHIERVA HUTTE

Round trip 25 km, 15½ miles
Hiking time 4 hours up, 3 down
High point 2573 meters, 8439 feet
Elevation gain 799 meters, 2620 feet
Map Julier Pass 268 or Wanderkarte Bernina

A hike up the Roseg River Valley to the Tschierva Hutte is very worthwhile because of its views. Also, it is one of the best places in the Grisons region to see marmots and chamois — the elusive mountain antelope which is the symbol of the Alps.

The trail starts near the railroad station in Pontresina, 1774 meters. Walk toward town for about 100 meters; next to the bridge over the Roseg River is a sign marked "Hotel Roseg." From here, you can either walk up the right side of the valley, on a dirt road used only by horse carriages and an occasional delivery truck, or on the left side of the river, on a very busy footpath. Either way is easy, with a vertical climb of only 200 meters for 7 km.

Just before reaching the Hotel Roseg, close to where the road crosses the river, the Tschierva Hutte trail can be found on the left bank. The trail follows the flat, wide valley for another kilometer and then starts up in earnest. As the trail climbs the views unfold: first the Roseg Glacier, then the Tschierva Glacier dominated by Mont Roseg. Within sight of the hut, the trail follows a gully between the lateral moraine and the hillside. At one point you can climb onto the moraine itself. The view is definitely better up there, but the moraine is sloughing away and the trail makes several detours. So it is best to continue in the gully, even though you may be obliged to cross patches of snow.

The Tschierva Hutte, perched at 2573 meters, is operated by the Swiss Alpine Club and offers meals and dormitory accommodations on a first-come, first-served basis. For even better views of the mountains it is worthwhile to climb above the hut. Chamois are most frequently seen at dusk or in early morning, many hours before the crowds of hikers scare them away. The chamois are protected here and consequently are not overly nervous. Sometimes they will completely ignore a person who is sitting quietly by the side of the trail and will come within easy camera range. However, marmots, who make their homes in burrows next to trails, under rocks, and in hillside holes, often let loose a shrill whistle when strangers approach.

There are several other worthwhile hikes from the Roseg Valley. For example, at the junction near the Hotel Roseg a trail goes for 5 km to the Coaz Hutte at 2610 meters, where there are dramatic views of Roseg Glacier. For one of the greatest views of the Bernina Mountains, you can climb 4 km to Surlej Pass, 2755 meters, and then go 8 km downhill to St. Moritz.

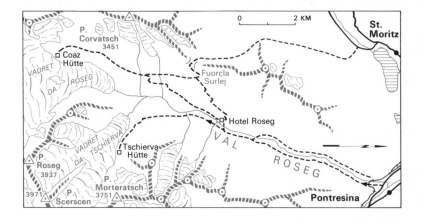

Ibex on side of Piz Languard

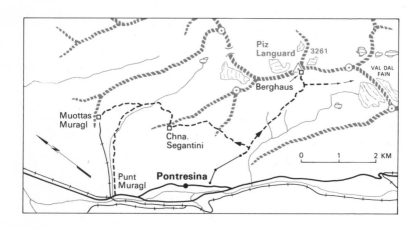

45 PIZ LANGUARD

Round trip 8 km, 5 miles
Hiking time 5 hours
High point 3262 meters, 10,699 feet
Elevation gain 1000 meters, 3280 feet
Map Berninapass 269

Bernina Range from Berghaus Piz Languard

A double dividend is the prize: dramatic views of the Bernina Range, and one of the best chances in the Alps to see the ibex, a species of wild goat that was almost extinct 60 years ago and now flourishes around Piz Languard and certain other areas in the Alps.

From the resort city of Pontresina, hike or ride to the upper terminal of the Languard chair lift, elevation 2280 meters. Above the lift, follow the "Piz Languard" signs. The trail climbs steadily and approximately halfway to the top it crosses a stream. A little farther it enters a nature preserve and switchbacks up the steep hillsides. At about 2900 meters, the Piz Languard trail meets another trail that goes to the Val dal Fain. Keep left, and be especially careful that you do not lose the faint path when crossing the frequent snow patches. Finally, the trail reaches Berghaus Piz Languard, a 3200-meter-high hotel and restuarant where reservations are necessary if you want to remain overnight. Continue past the hotel to the summit, which is 61 meters higher.

It is more interesting to descend into the valley by a different route. One good possibility is to go via the Val dal Fain; another takes you by way of the Chamanna Segantini restaurant to Muottas Muragl and down to the railroad tracks. From there you can easily reach Pontresina.

Hoping to photograph the ibex, we took this hike early in the summer, keeping our cameras ready at every turn of the trail. We did see a lone chamois; but that wasn't what we were looking for. At the Berghaus Piz Languard we were told that in June and July the big male ibex live in the rocky outcroppings lower on the mountain. They only move to higher ground in August and September. So, after soaking up the views, we hiked down; sure enough, a short distance above the chair lift we found four males grazing. Since they are not hunted, they are unafraid of man, and we were able to approach them. Like all mountain animals, the ibex is best observed early in the morning or at dusk.

46 MORTERATSCH GLACIER

Round trip 8 km, 5 miles
Hiking time 4 hours
High point 2495 meters, 8184 feet
Elevation gain 600 meters, 1986 feet
Map Julierpass 268, Berninapass 269

This hike runs along a glacier to a mountain hut with marvelous views of glaciers and peaks. In season, the trail is banked with lovely alpine rose; this scene, with flowers in the foreground and glacier in the background, has often been photographed for use in travel brochures and calendars.

From Pontresina, the trail can be reached by a short railroad or car trip to Morteratsch. Either way, go 5 km toward Bernina Pass, to the Morteratsch railroad station. Directly in front of the station is a trail sign on a gated service road, elevation 1896 meters. Hike on this road for a few hundred meters, then follow the trail to the right, switchbacking up a forested hillside which gains 200 meters in 1 km. The trail levels a bit, then leaves the forest to traverse a steep hillside. This is the place to get out your camera, because 500 meters farther, views are obscured by a high lateral moraine. At about 3 km, the trail leaves the moraine and again steepens as it climbs a knoll; at 4 km, it reaches the Swiss Alpine Club's Boval hut at 2495 meters.

The meadow in front of the hut is an ideal place to stretch out and enjoy the scenery or have lunch, which the hutkeeper will serve you. Directly across from the hut, the Pers Glacier flows into the Morteratsch Glacier and a whole circle of glacier-covered peaks unfolds: Piz Bernina, Piz Zupp, Piz Palu, and Piz Cambrena. Piz Boval is directly behind the hut.

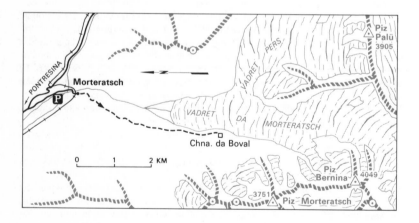

Morteratsch Glacier

47 AUGSTENBERG

Loop trip 10 km, 6 miles
Hiking time 5 hours
High point 2359 meters, 7738 feet
Elevation gain 800 meters, 2624 feet
Map Liechtenstein Wanderkarte

Considering that Liechtenstein consists of only 157 square km, the principality has an impressive number of good hikes. Solitude on the trails is not unsuual, although that is not the case in the hike up the Augstenberg. A chair lift has opened up the area and walkers are making use of it. Nevertheless, hikers disdaining these mechanical contraptions can always exercise their option of climbing all the way.

From the capital city of Vaduz, where 3000 hardy persons make up the population, go by autobus or car on the road marked "Steg." From Steg continue to the road's end at Malbun, elevation 1602 meters. You can either hike up the service road to the 2000-meter-high Sareiser-Joch (pass) or ride up on the chair lift. If you hike up, the route is obvious: look for the lowest point on the ridge and point yourself in that direction. Once on top of the ridge, follow it south, then west, as it curves around the bowl-shaped valley above Malbun. With more ups than downs, the trail follows near the ridge crest, climbing over and around limestone outcroppings. At 3½ km it reaches the 2359-meter-high Augstenberg. From the 100-meter-high bluff you will have fine views of the Gamperdona Valley in Austria, the tiny farm village of Nenzinger-Himmel, and some Swiss summits in the Graubunden (Grissons) canton.

At this point you can retrace your steps and return to the valley, or continue along the ridge trail southward, contouring into Austria to the Pfalzer-Hutte at the Bettlerjoch, elevation 2108 meters, and the meeting of five trails, a good place to spend the night. The following day there is plenty to do. You can explore the trail leading south to Naafkopf where Austria, Liechtenstein, and Switzerland share a common border, or follow the ridge trail eastward to Salarueljoch.

If you must return to Malbun the same day, take the trail that heads west, toward Gritsch, from the five-trail junction. This trail is just below the ridge you arrived on. After

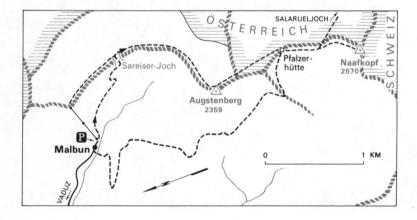

Town of Malbun from Augstenberg

rounding the first major corner, the trail descends slightly; at 6½ km there is a junction. Remain high on the trail that turns around the Augstenberg. At 9½ km, cross a bridge above Malbun, and join a service road which leads back to the village.

111

48 HEUBUHL-RAPPENSTEIN RIDGE TRAIL

Round trip to Heubuhl 8 km, 5 miles
Hiking time 3 hours
High point 1936 meters, 6352 feet
Elevation gain 333 meters, 1092 feet

Round trip to Rappenstein 12 km, 7½ miles
Hiking time 4½ hours
High point 2222 meters, 7290 feet
Elevation gain 819 meters, 2687 feet
Map Liechtenstein Wanderkarte

This difficult trail along a sharp ridge offers breathtaking views of the Rhine River Valley on one side and a pretty alpine valley on the other. In many places the trail is narrow, faint, and completely ungraded; you will frequently find yourself clambering over slippery roots and rocks or easing yourself along narrow pathways on fall-away cliffs. However, keep your calm. The views are worth the effort, and you are very likely to find solitude.

From the city of Vaduz travel out of the Rhine Valley by bus or car 11½ km toward Steg. Shortly after leaving a tunnel, just before the village of Steg, you arrive at a large parking lot and bus stop on the left, elevation 1303 meters. The hike starts there. Walk across the Samina River bridge and follow the paved road towards Sucka. After 1 km or 20 minutes' walking you will reach a fork; keep right. The left trail goes to the Sucka Hotel and on up the valley; you may wish to return this way. Continue on the right trail until you come to a tunnel where you will find several trail signs pointing in at least three directions. Your trail is to the left, marked "Heubuhl-Wang-Lawena Triesen."

The trail starts off as an old farm road, staying nearly level as it passes through fields of flowers, then through sparse woods. After the woods you pass into a large field again. Head up toward a low spot at the far end of the field or at whatever point seems easiest

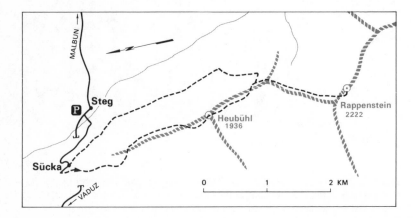

to you; once there, you will find an ill defined path marked with red and white paint stripes. At the end of the pasture, start through forest up a series of progressively high rises along the ridgetop; the second major rise is the Heubuhl, 1936 meters. From Heubuhl onward the forest gives way to lush meadow, bright red in July with alpine rose. The trail splits and becomes indistinct on reaching the meadows. The marked trail traverses the hill on the Samina River side before heading up to the summit. If you miss the trail, continue to the high point of the hill where you will rejoin it.

From the top of Heubuhl, approximately 4 km from the parking area, the views are magnificent. Nearly 1200 meters below you are what appear to be the toy villages of Liechtenstein and Switzerland, with tiny cars and buses dashing here and there. The views of the mountains at the end of the Samina River Valley are themselves worth the trip.

If you still have some energy, follow the ridgetop to the next rise, the Wanghohe, then down to a trail crossing, and up another rise; then take the long climb over green slopes to the Rappenstein, a 2222-meter-high summit. On your return trip you can make a loop: go down the extremely steep trail after the Wanghohe, on the Samina Valley side, to a road visible below at 1623 meters. You can then walk back to the Sucka Hotel on a good road. This ridge trip is rough and narrow in places. Don't try it when visibility is poor, or on rainy days.

Rhine Valley from Heubuhl-Rappenstein Ridge

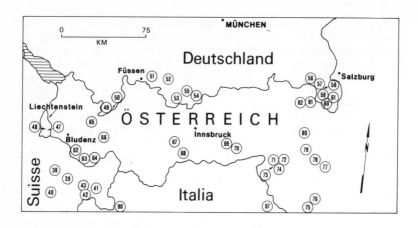

St. Bartholoma and Konigssee (Hike No. 61)

GERMANY - DEUTSCHLAND

49 ROSSGUNDKOPF LOOP Strenuous 1-day or good overnight loop trip in alpine meadows, crossing a high pass, to see views and chamois. Near Oberstdorf.

50 OBER GAISALPSEE Day hike through alpine farms to a small lake. Alternatively, cable car ride up and walk down. From Oberstdorf.

51 TEGELBERG A castle, a summit, and forest trails are features of a day loop trip. Near Fussen.

52 KLAMMSPITZ Step trail to a summit with panoramic views; long day trip. Near Oberammergau.

53 REINTALANGERHUTTE Following a mountain stream to an alpine hut, day trip in forest. Starts at Garmisch-Partenkirchen.

54 SOIERNSEE Long day or overnight loop trip over a high pass to two alpine lakes. Near Mittenwald.

55 HOHE KISTEN Alpine meadows and views reached on a steep forest trail; 1 day. Near Mittenwald.

56 VORDERER KRAXENBACH ALM Easy day hike in a narrow valley to a waterfall. Near Bad Reichenhall.

57 SONNTAGSHORN Long, steep day hike to a 1961-meter peak on the German-Austrian border, with panoramic views. Near Bad Reichenhall.

58 REITER ALPE High plateau with interesting rock formations reached in 1 or more days. Near Berchtesgaden.

59 BLAUEIS HUTTE Day hike through forest to a mountain hut. Near Berchtesgaden.

60 WIMBACHGRIESHUTTE Hike in a wide valley bordered by pinnacles and crags; 1-2 days. Near Berchtesgaden.

61 KONIGSSEE Boat ride, then a spectacular climb high above the Konigssee; return by trail to the starting point. Long day trip. Near Berchtesgaden.

A stag grazing near the Kuhrointhaus (Hike No. 61)

49 ROSSGUNDKOPF LOOP

Loop trip 15 km, 9½ miles
Hiking time 10 hours
High point 2005 meters, 6575 feet
Elevation gain 800 meters, 2624 feet
Map Kompass Wanderkarte 3

This 2-day hike is strenuous but well worth the effort. You hike around a peak of eroded limestone with views of snowcapped summits and the deep glacier-carved Rappenalpental Valley. There is a good chance to see many wildflowers, deer, and chamois.

From Oberstdorf follow the signs to the Fellhornbahn cable car. If you object to gaining elevation by mechanical means, follow trail 443 starting near the cable car terminal. The hike is partly on road, partly on trail. It climbs 840 meters.

Chamois on side of the Fellhorn

We took the tram to the middle station, elevation 1780 meters. However, on a clear day it would be worthwhile to start from the top station, where there are fine views toward the east into Austria's Kleines Walsertal. From the rear of the mid-station, find a trail marked with purple and red stakes. The trail drops slightly and then contours southward. At 1 km, the trail goes under the cables of a chair lift; then, with ups and downs, it passes a second set of cables, and, climbing and descending, it contours on. At 4 km, elevation 1744 meters, you reach the Kuhgund Alpe, where a fork in the trail requires a decision The right trail climbs steeply to a 2150-meter pass and offers a short side trip to the Fiderpass Hutte; the left trail climbs over even steeper ground through the 2005-meter-high Rossgund-Scharte Pass. On the day we hiked, the higher pass was in the clouds, so we went left and were glad we did: we spotted a dozen chamois close to the trail.

Although the left trail starts out gently, it soon becomes very steep, climbing 260 meters in 1 km. At approximately 5 km from the start, you reach Rossgund-Scharte, where the view opens up to peaks across the valley. From there the trail contours south and descends. At 6½ km it meets the upper trail, and at 7 km there is a second junction. Most hikers continue another 3 km to the Mindelheimer Hutte where they spend the night. The next day they descend to the valley and then walk along a gated farm road back to the starting point.

We took another trail down. It's considerably shorter, but more difficult. Follow trail 442, signed "Birgsau." It is seldom used and in places is so obscure you must look carefully for the paint marks. With considerable ups and downs, the trail goes north past tiny Guggersee at 9½ km, and shortly after begins to fall steeply to the road at Birgsau at 13 km. It's then level walking for a total of 15 km.

After that knee-shaking descent, we were convinced that it is preferable to stay overnight in the mountains and hike the easier trail back to Oberstdorf the next day.

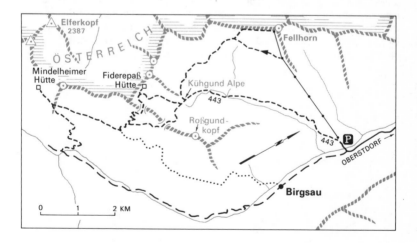

50 OBER GAISALPSEE

Round trip 18 km, 11 miles
Hiking time 6 hours
High point 1650 meters, 5412 feet
Elevation gain 840 meters, 2756 feet
Map Kompass Wanderkarte 3

This area, which can be reached by trail or cable car, is perfect for wandering. The high alpine meadows are spotted with small, whitish limestone boulders and outcroppings often weathered into odd shapes. Sharp cliffs and jagged peaks are interspersed with grassy summits which tempt the hiker to leave the trail and explore farther.

From the top of the Nebelhorn cable car you can hike a variety of routes and trails which make interesting loop hikes. Engeratsgundsee and Seealpsee are two such trips. For that reason, most people go up the cable car. However, the hike is more challenging if you begin in the valley.

In Oberstdorf, elevation 810 meters, follow the signs to Nebelhornbahn. From there take the first turn left, and cross a bridge which brings you to the public parking lot. Walk to the far end of the lot, and follow the signs through the city park to Gaisalpe. Continue up the road. After several twists and turns, take the trail off to the left. At 500 meters you pass Cafe Breitenberg, and then traverse a forest on the lower slopes of the Rubihorn. At 5¼ km, you arrive at a major junction where you meet the trail from Rubi, and, shortly thereafter, the trail from Reichenbach.

A short steep climb brings you to Gaisalpe, 1149 meters, 6 km from the start, where there is a popular restaurant and cafe. The trail continues on its steep, wet, and slippery way up the hill, switchbacking and scrambling over rocky hillsides until at 7½ km it arrives at Unter Gaisalpsee (Lower Gaisalpe Lake), 1550 meters, surrounded by meadows and forests. The trail continues 100 meters higher to the Ober Gaisalpsee in much the same manner as before—steep switchbacks on a rugged, rocky, slippery trail. Like its counterpart below, the Ober Gaisalpsee is a small alpine lake nestled in a slight depression surrounded by meadows. The views of stately peaks and the valley below

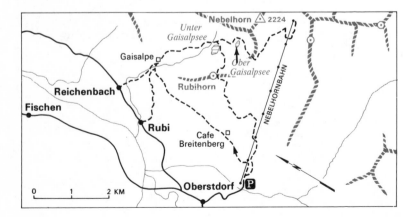

Unter Gaisalpsee

are more impressive from this upper lake. Scramble up to any of the nearby ridgetops for even better, unobstructed, views. At 1650 meters, this is a good place to call it a day.

An interesting variation on your return from the lower lake is the ambitious hike up the Rubihorn, an elevation gain of 400 meters. Your reward for this steep climb is the shorter distance back to Oberstdorf. But whether you climb to the summit or go down the main trail, do not expect a quick return. The trail is rugged and nearly as difficult to walk down as it was to climb up.

The trip to Ober Gaisalpsee can also be made from the top of the Nebelhorn cable car. Follow a rugged but pretty trail down to the lake for approximately 2½ km, and then return to Oberstdorf via Gaisalpe or Rubihorn.

Neuschwanstein Castle

51 TEGELBERG

Loop trip 15 km, 9½ miles
Hiking time 7 hours
High point 1707 meters, 5599 feet
Elevation gain 900 meters, 2952 feet
Map Kompass Wanderkarte 4

Tegelberg and its marvels are not far from the city of Fussen in the Bavarian Alps. Although there is a cable lift on the mountain, hundreds of sturdy tourists climb up and down the trails to see and visit Neuschwanstein Castle, the gorge, waterfalls, forests, chamois, the fascinating limestone formations, and—from the summit itself—an aerial view of lakes, farms, and villages.

The trail starts near the village of Hohenschwangau. From the parking lot walk up the road a short distance, and find a broad path with a sign indicating the castle (schloss) and the Tegelberg. Once on the trail, you will notice that there are several left-hand trails which branch off to the castle. That is where most of the tourists go. We went straight ahead. After 1 km cross a roaring waterfall on a high footbridge. The trail narrows and begins a seemingly endless series of switchbacks. At first the castle can be seen through the trees; but then the trail turns a corner and the views are toward the south. The hillside gets steeper. The trail climbs between pillars of limestone; the metal handrail is a welcome aid.

At approximately 3½ km, elevation 1300 meters, the trail levels off, drops a few meters, and then climbs again. At 5 km there is a fork. Both steep trails head for the summit, but the right-hand trail is somewhat shorter. If the weather is good, the views from the summit platform are spectacular. A thousand vertical meters below lie farms, lakes, and cities looking much the way they looked in the 19th century.

From the summit, take the trail heading southeast toward the Ahornsattel. At 1 km is a trail junction. The shortest way is to keep right. However, for the best views, detour to the left over Ahornsattel and rejoin the main trail in 1½ km. Either way in enjoyable. The meadows are rich, the forests thick, and herds of chamois live in the rocks and feed in this area. At 4 km the trail widens into a gravel road, traverses dense forests, parallels a river, and is very idyllic. But at 7½ km, the river dramatically plunges through a steep gorge from which one has an astonishing view of Neuschwanstein Castle. Its many spires and turrets rise high in the air, and it is hard to believe one is living in the 20th century. The road climbs a bit; at the top of the hill, take the path toward the footbridge, and the loop around the Tegelberg is complete.

Even though you add another kilometer to the hike, it is worthwhile to explore the gorge from the vantage point of a catwalk which is bolted to the cliffs. From the footbridge, walk to within 200 meters of the castle, and find an unmarked path leading down into the gorge to the river. Follow this path downstream. Sometimes you are at the edge of the water and sometimes suspended only a meter or two above the torrent.

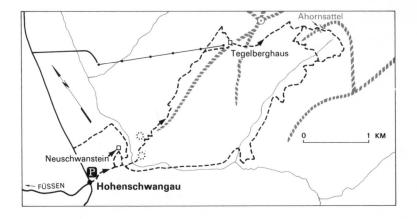

GERMANY

Shoulder of Klammspitz

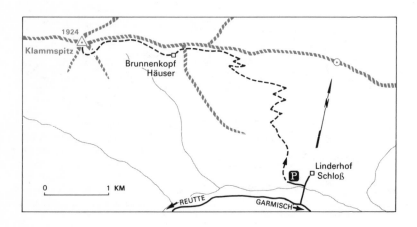

52 KLAMMSPITZ

Round trip 20 km, 12½ miles
Hiking time 6 hours up, 3 down
High point 1882 meters, 6173 feet
Elevation gain 1040 meters, 3411 feet
Map Kompass Wanderkarte 5

Hikers on summit of Klammspitz

On a good weekend hundreds of hikers, including small children tied up to their fathers by short ropes, climb the highest summit of the Klammspitz, 1882 meters. It's a Bavarian specialty, like the passion plays at the city of Oberammergau, about 15 km distant.

Even though it is popular, it is not an easy trip. It is fairly long and strenuous; and on the final pitches, the trail peters out. The summit push more nearly resembles a rock scramble than a Sunday outing with the grandparents. The climb to the summit should definitely be avoided on wet days.

From highway 23 between Oberammergau and Garmisch-Partenkirchen, turn west toward Reutte and travel to the Linderhof Schloss (castle). On the west side of the castle parking lot is a small stream. Cross the bridge and follow the stream to the trailhead (elevation 960 meters). The trail, which is a steep wagon road, bridges the stream a couple of times, and at approximately 1 km it crosses a well developed forest road. Shortly thereafter it begins to double back and forth through the forest, and at 4½ km it reaches the meadows, where there are several small farmhouses. The views are imposing. At 1602 meters, ½ km farther, you reach the small Brunnenkopf Hauser restaurant where the wagon road ends and a narrow trail leads up to a mountain saddle. From the saddle one gets the first closeup view of the Klammspitz. The trail leading up the mountain appears to be a lot steeper than it really is. It contours around a steep hillside, losing about 100 meters' altitude in the process, and then winds back and forth to a second saddle, comes around a buttress of the mountain, and climbs up the back side over rocks.

In addition to the fine panoramic views, we saw two chamois. The first one was lying down less than 100 meters from the trail; the second on an overhanging cliff, was showing off his climbing skills to an appreciative audience of tired hikers.

53 REINTALANGERHUTTE

Round trip 28 km, 17½ miles
Hiking time 7½ hours
High point 1367 meters, 4484 feet
Elevation gain 567 meters, 1860 feet
Map Kompass Wanderkarte 5

This is a long, pleasant hike up a beautiful narrow valley walled in by peaks whose sheer rock faces rise straight up from the valley floor. Paralleling a rushing stream most of the way, the trail passes through a narrow canyon, past a lake and a waterfall, and through thick forest before reaching open meadows. Along the entire trail are splendid views and, as a bonus, there is very little elevation gain.

In Garmisch-Partenkirchen, drive or take the town bus in the direction of Mittenwald to the Skistadion (ski stadium). If you are arriving in Garmisch-Partenkirchen by train, get off at the Kainzenbad station and walk to the Skistadion (elevation 800 meters), from which you then walk along a paved road. In tourist season, you'll have no trouble finding the way: just follow the crowds. Horse-drawn buggies offer taxi service for those who need it. At Wildenau (1½ km), the paved road ends. After that cross a bridge, turn right, and follow the paved trail marked Partnachklamm. This trail parallels the river a short distance, then divides. The lower route, a toll trail, has been hacked out of the sheer canyon walls and frequently passes through dark tunnels. If you take the lower trail, it's fascinating to watch the river as it twists and rolls down a narrow channel. The canyon is damp and waterfalls come off both sides. Besides being very interesting, this trail has the advantage of staying at river level.

However, if you don't wish to pay the toll, you can avoid it. At the trail division just before the tollgate, take the trail heading steeply uphill, from which there are several good views into the canyon. At 3 km, the trail joins a dirt road going toward the Reintalangerhutte, paralleling the Partnach River. The walk is made interesting by frequent views of the mountains ahead. At 7½ km the road ends, and the real trail through forests begins. The valley is narrower now, boxed in by steep cliffs topped by rugged, barren peaks. At 9 km the trail to Schachenhaus branches off to the left. Shortly

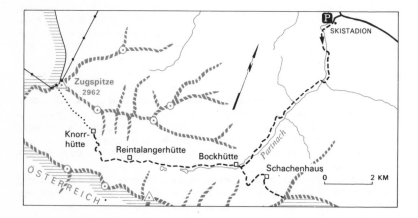

Vord Blaue Gumpe, a shallow lake in the Reintal (valley)

beyond is Bockhutte. The trail, formerly signed "R 1," is now "R 2" or "801." After Bockhutte the forest thins and the views are sensational.

At 11½ km, the river is blocked by the talus and debris of rock slides from the peaks above, forming several shallow lakes. The trail passes by the first lake (a good rest stop); at 13 km, it climbs over a waterfall into green meadows. About 1 km farther you arrive at the Reintalangerhutte, 1367 meters high, ready for a good rest.

If energy, time, and weather permit, consider going to the Knorr-Hutte, elevation gain 684 meters. The hut, in the lower part of a rocky basin, is surrounded by tall peaks including the Zugspitz, 2962 meters, Germany's highest mountain.

125

54 SOIERNSEE

Loop trip 17 km, 10½ miles
Hiking time 10 hours
High point 2050 meters, 6725 feet
Elevation gain 1183 meters, 3880 feet
Map Kompass Wanderkarte 5

This is a steep loop hike in forest to high open meadows, rugged peaks, and hair-raising walks across razor-sharp saddles to a pair of lovely lakes.

By bus or auto take highway 11 between Mittenwald and Walchensee to the town of Krun. There, turn right at the church, going in the direction of Soierngebiet. At the intersection just behind the church, follow the street called Fischbachalmstrasse. Find a parking space near a dry river bed, elevation 875 meters. Walk across the bridge, turn left, and walk on the road for a short 100 meters. Take the first signed path on the right heading uphill.

The trail soon comes out on an overgrown logging road and follows it a short distance. Head left, following the signs to Seinskopf and Schottelkarspitze. Red dots mark the way. For the first 1½ km, the way climbs up through thick second-growth timber; then it goes around the mountain, staying relatively level. At 2 km there is a viewpoint of Krun and a neatly-farmed valley. The trail climbs steeply, sometimes by switchback, more often by heading straight uphill toward a tall rock wall. Near the base of the wall it turns left, climbing and traversing until at 4 km it comes to a junction just above Felsenkopf, 1562 meters. At 4½ km, the trail arrives at a ridge crest with views of two immense peaks, the Schottelkarspitze and the Schottelkopf. Most striking are the bands of limestone extending from peak to peak.

The trail follows the ridge crest until it switchbacks up the final slope to a high saddle, Am Seinskopf, at 1956 meters. Bursting into view is a massive group of rock peaks including Worner, 2476 meters; Hochkarspitze, 2484 meters; and Tiefkarspitze, 2430 meters. The vegetation is now high alpine with short grass and flowers. In every direction the descent is steep.

Continue toward Schottelkarspitze, dropping 100 meters across another saddle, climbing very steeply up to Feldernkreuz, crossing a very narrow saddle with sheer

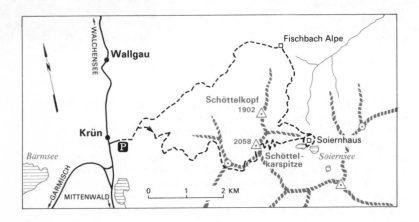

Soiernsee from Schottelkarspitze

drop-offs on either side. This final bit is rather nerve-wracking and should be attempted only in good weather.

At 6½ km you arrive at the summit of Schottelkarspitze, 2050 meters. From the peak descend to the Soiernhaus, 1613 meters, 8 km, a hut where you can spend the night overlooking the two Soiernsee lakes. Unfortunately, camping is forbidden.

From the lakes, follow the trail which traverses the hillside without any major descents to Fieshbach Alpe, 12 km, elevation 1402 meters. Pass in front of a hut and start downhill on an unmarked trail to a steep service road that takes you back to the starting point.

55 HOHE KISTEN

Round trip 16 km, 10 miles
Hiking time 6 hours
High point 1650 meters, 5412 feet
Elevation gain 800 meters, 2624 feet
Map Kompass Wanderkarte 5

If it is just ravishing scenery you want, take the cable car from Garmisch-Parten-kirchen. The trail, however, offers solitude, a lovely forest, meadows, and a magnificent view from the 1922-meter-high Hohe Kisten.

The map shows many interesting trails in this area. However, some of them have been replaced by a new system of forest roads; others have been destroyed by logging operations, so only a few remain and these are not well marked.

Go by bus or auto to Wallgau on highway 11 between Mittenwald and Walchen. About 1 km north of town find a forest road on the west side, signed "Krottenkopf" and "Simetsberg." Follow the forest road to a gate and park there (elevation 850 meters). In 1 km there is a junction; take the uphill fork. At 3 km, cross a stream, leave the road, and take the trail climbing steeply up the right side of the stream. The trail is first wide then becomes a narrow footpath, climbing 300 meters in a little more than 1 km. Then the grade slackens off and at 1392 meters, 4½ km, reaches the tiny Wildsee surrounded by green marshy meadows. From there the trail becomes very obscure, but the way is obvious, climbing up a ravine passing through open glades and forest. At 8 km, the ravine ends on a low ridge at Kuhalm, elevation 1650 meters, an alpine meadow with a farmhouse. Above the meadow is Hohe Kisten, a high point with a large cross on top. The meadow is a great place to sit and decide whether to go on or to explore some of the trails shown on the topographic map.

If you are going on, cross the meadow at Kuhalm and pick up a service road which soon becomes a trail contouring under Hohe Kisten. A short distance beyond is a scramble path to the cross and viewpoint. If you have come this far you should continue on to a well deserved overnight stay at Krottenkoph Hutte. The following day, take a short walk to the top of Krottenkoph, 2086 meters high, 8 km from Wallgau.

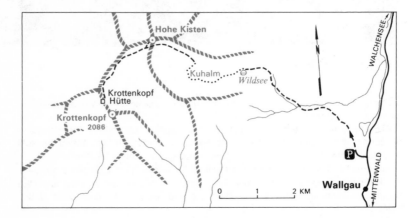

Tiny Wildsee

Instead of going to the top, we decided to explore some of the trails shown on the map. If you enjoy exploring as much as we do, give it a try. Just be careful not to end up in the valley going toward Garmisch, a long way from the starting point.

Some areas are notable for their deer, others for chamois, birds, or the views; but the Hohe Kisten area must be noted for its ants. There were dozens of huge anthills along the trail.

56 VORDERER KRAXENBACH ALM

Round trip 11 km, 7 miles
Hiking time 5 hours
High point 1400 meters, 4593 feet
Elevation gain 650 meters, 2120 feet
Map Kompass Wanderkarte 12

Waterfall near Vorderer Kraxenbach Alm

Here is a short steep trail to a waterfall and a pretty meadow surrounded by high ridges running out of the Sonntagshorn, 1981 meters, and Hirscheck, 1901 meters. This storybook meadow is very green, with many flowers. A little cabin is situated at the edge of the meadow, overlooking the narrow forested valley and a high green hill beyond. It's the ideal picnic spot.

Take a bus or drive to Laubau, a small village on highway 305 between Reit im Winkl and Bad Reichenhall. Park in the public parking lot, elevation 750 meters. The hike starts up a gated forest road with the first ¾ km paved. After crossing a dry stream bed, the way becomes gravel and follows the bed uphill. At 1 km you pass an unmarked junction; stay at stream level. At 1½ km the road rounds a big bend and follows the stream, which now has water in it. At about 3 km you reach Schwarzachenalm, where there is a covered picnic area and drinking water.

At Schwarzachenalm, just short of the picnic area, turn right, leave the road, and head up a side valley. Follow the signs to Sonntagshorn. The trail parallels the Danzingbach stream up a narrow valley for 1 km to a trail division. Take the right fork, trail 37, which crosses the river and heads up a still narrower side valley; the trail steepens as it goes across and up this new valley paralleling the Mittler Krazanbach stream. At 2 km the trail crosses the stream and continues up the other side of the valley. Be sure to stay on the correct trail.

After leaving the valley floor, the trail, sometimes narrow and slippery, climbs steeply 500 meters through thick forest to the Alm. It parallels a fast-moving creek and a waterfall.

The forest starts to thin out and the trail passes through several glades. One can look up to see rocky ridges towering several hudred meters above on both sides of the valley. About 2½ km beyond Schwarzachenalm, the trail passes a second waterfall; shortly above is the Vorderer Kraxenbach Alm, where you can break out the picnic basket.

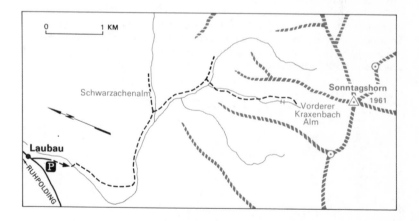

Sign near top of Sonntagshorn

57 SONNTAGSHORN

Round trip 16 km, 10 miles
Hiking time 9 hours
High point 1961 meters, 6432 feet
Elevation gain 1403 meters, 4601 feet
Map Kompass Wanderkarte 12

This is a long grueling climb to high alpine meadows and then to the summit of the Sonntagshorn. The peak is guarded by a series of short wall-like cliffs formed from steeply dipping beds of limestone. Although trails approach the peak from all directions, only this one does not involve rock climbing.

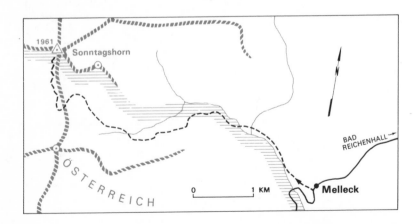

From Bad Reichenhall, take highway 21 south towards Steinpass on the German-Austrian border. Leave the bus or park your car at Melleck. Take the path behind the hotel-restaurant at the edge of town, and walk down the hill toward Austria for 250 meters until you reach a forest road. Another possibility is to walk down the main road ½ km and take the first turn to the left, just after the sign announcing the Austrian frontier.

The trail starts up a gravel logging road paralleling the Steinbach River. The valley is narrow and steeply forested hills rise sharply on both sides. The climbing begins at 1½ km, when the road ends. Cross a wooden bridge over the Vorderer Steinbach (stream), climb a steep incline, then level off and follow the signs to the Sonntagshorn. The trail appears to have been long abandoned, then partially renovated. You can get through, but occasionally the way is very narrow. Red and white painted stripes mark the trail, which switchbacks and traverses rapidly up steep wooded slopes. Views are poor as the trail crosses the Rosskar Bach (stream) at 4 km, and then passes a logged clearing containing a workman's hut. At 4½ km the trail enters open meadows and becomes indistinct. However, you have the painted trail marks to follow. Head up into the meadows until you reach a small farm road; follow it to the left up to the ridgetop.

For those who have had enough after 6 km, the ridgetop at 1650 meters is a fine turnaround point. Views from here are nearly as good as those from the summit, and it is very pleasant just to wander along the crest and do some dreaming.

For the courageous, however, the trail continues to the right on the ridge. The route goes up open slopes and through stunted pines, and is steep, with innumerable switchbacks. However, 2 km bring you to the summit at 1961 meters, 8 km from the start, where you will no doubt feel a sense of accomplishment. There are broad views into Austria as well as Germany, with Reiter Alpe to the southeast and the Loferer and Leoganger Stenberge to the south.

Anemones

58 REITER ALPE

Round trip 14 km, 9 miles
Hiking time 6½ hours
High point 1557 meters, 5107 feet
Elevation gain 607 meters, 1991 feet
Map Wanderkarte 14

The Reiter Alpe, split by the unseen line of the German-Austrian border, is an intriguing area in which to spend a day or a week. On the topographic map it appears to be a level plateau raised by towering 1000-meter cliffs above the surrounding farmlands. This is almost correct: the plateau is by no means level. Instead, the area is characterized by depressions, with steep sides and high peaks. Terrain is extremely

Eroded rock in Reiter Alp

rugged, made so by the predominance of rock rather than vegetation. Meadows are spotted by extremely weathered white and pink limestone boulders and outcroppings. Many appear to have had water running across them in the distant past, creating long, narrow, parallel grooves.

The German part of the Alpe is quite rugged; toward the Austrian border lush meadows with rounder hills are dominant. The views are splendid, and the possibilities for wandering around the area start near the Neue Traunsteiner Hutte.

Apart from the occasional loud detonations from the German army's firing range in the northeast section of the Alps, the area is peaceful. You will, however, want to heed the signs that warn hikers not to enter the danger zone.

To reach Reiter Alpe, travel by bus or car on highway 305 between Bad Reichenhall and Berchtesgaden to the hamlet of Schwarsbachwacht, elevation 950 meters. At the Berchtesgaden end of the village, turn right onto the road towards Ramsau and Hintersee; park on the right side, immediately after the turn. Walk around behind the building to the left of the parking area and continue straight ahead to a small abandoned road. From there you cannot get lost if you follow the signs to Neue Traunsteiner Hutte, also called Karl-Merkensschlager-haus.

Follow the road as it heads gently downhill behind the town. Step over the cow gate, and take the well signed road forking to the left. At the next fork go left again. After 1 km, the trail begins, climbing uphill with switchbacks. It is narrow and rough, and the rocks and roots are slippery. After approximately 4 km and a long series of false summits, the trail arrives at a small glen with several old ruined buildings and a flagpole. Here is the first sign warning the hiker not to wander off the trail to the north. Continue over a series of rises and short descents. At approximately 6 km, the views of mountains which form the rim of the Alpe begin to appear. At 7 km, you will be in an open valley with the Neue Traunsteiner Hutte on the German side of the frontier and the Alte Traunsteiner Hutte on the Austrian side.

Whether you stay overnight in the new or the old hut, in Austria or Germany, many trails take off toward the rim peaks. All offer sensational views, but this is an area you will want to explore with care because of the terrain.

Be sure to allow plenty of time for the return trip. The trail is rough and the descent into the valley requires almost as much time as the climb up.

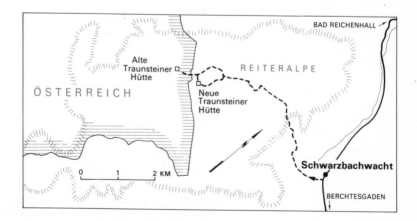

135

59 BLAUEIS HUTTE

Round trip 10 km, 6 miles
Hiking time 5 hours
High point 1750 meters, 5740 feet
Elevation gain 1000 meters, 3280 feet
Map Kompass Wanderkarte 14

Restaurant at Scharten Alm

The action of the glaciers is best seen on this hike, which takes you from a valley bottom through forests to another valley, this one very steep and glacier-scoured.

Take a bus or drive on highway 305 from Berchtesgaden to the town of Ramsau. On the outskirts of town, 500 meters beyond the Post Office, cross a stream on a one-lane bridge and park in the lot, elevation 750 meters. One trail starts there; there is a second trailhead 4 km farther, near Hintersee. Both trails are good and eventually join.

The trail starts as a wide, moderately steep forest road. At 800 meters, take a right fork on a steep wagon road. There are a number of well marked turnoffs, but stay on the wagon road until it ends. Then continue on a rocky trail that joins the second route, a

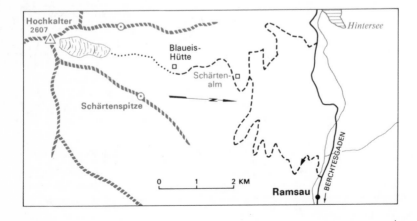

Alpine chalet near Blaueis Hutte

jeep road, from Hintersee. Follow this and at 3 km, 1362 meters, you reach the small restaurant at Scharten Alm. The trail levels off and even drops a few meters as it contours under cliffs and crosses a wooden bridge. At 4 km, the service road ends and the trail switchbacks up steeply to the Blaueis Hutte, 5 km, 1750 meters. This is base camp for mountain climbers and a good place to watch them in action.

To see the glacier, take a rocky trail 1 km farther. Although little ice remains, the immense boulders that have fallen off the surrounding cliffs, the huge tilted slabs of rock, and the large moraine are fascinating and attest to a once very active glacier.

60 WIMBACHGRIESHUTTE

Round trip 16 km, 10 miles
Hiking time 5 hours
High point 1327 meters, 4354 feet
Elevation gain 577 meters, 1893 feet
Map Kompass Wanderkarte 14

This is a popular hike along a graveled service road to the Wimbachgrieshutte, which is surrounded by peaks, pinnacles, and crags. The trip can be extended several days to include the Konigssee and scrambles to various mountaintops.

Take the autobus or drive to the village of Schwaben, located on highway 305 between Bad Reichenhall and Berchtesgaden. Find Wimbachweg (a road) and cross the Ramsauer Ache (river) on a single-lane car bridge. Directly across the bridge is a large parking lot, elevation 780 meters. Continue by foot on the same road and head uphill—the way is steep. As it leaves the village the paved road turns to gravel; after 500 meters or so, a trail takes off to the left going downhill to Wimbachklamm, while the road continues up the hill.

Wimbachklamm is a short side trip on a toll trail through a narrow gorge. The wood-planked walkway has been built out from the walls in order to give access to a waterfall, which emerges from a crack near the top of the cliff on the opposite side. The toll trail rejoins the road, which goes over the top of the gorge. At about 2 km, the road passes by a waterworks and the river disappears underground. From this point to the end of the valley the river is a broad gravel bed. However, the road offers very pleasant walking as it goes through forest; there are many benches for those who wish to stop, think, and dream. At 4 km is the Wimbachschloss, a former hunting lodge, elevation 937 meters, now a restaurant.

The road continues up the valley and the forest thins out. There are long sections crossing barren slide areas and the river bed. You are rewarded by views of peaks rising sharply from both sides of the valley. At 6 km, the road narrows to a path wide enough only for a small vehicle to carry supplies to the hut. The path heads around a turn in the valley and at 8 km arrives at Wimbachgrieshutte, 1327 meters. This cozy hut is located

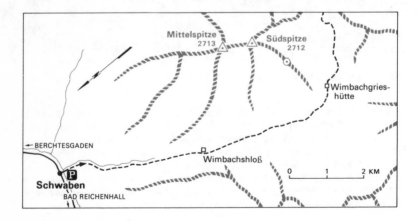

Curious deer at Wimbachgrieshutte

on an oasis of green amid barren peaks and river bed. A wide lawn and a forested hill give it a very park-like atmosphere. Fresh water is available from a pipe located at the top of the knoll beyond the hut.

The trip can be continued. There is a good trail from the hut over a relatively low pass, 1650 meters, at the end of the valley. After you cross the pass and start down the other side, there is a trail junction: the right fork goes to Funtensee, 1601 meters; take the left fork down to the Konigssee. The trail parallels the lake, and at 10 km from the hut arrives at St. Bartholoma, the site of a famous and beautiful monastery. From there take a boat back to Berchtesgaden, where you catch a bus for the short return trip to the starting point.

St. Bartholoma and the Konigssee

61 KONIGSSEE

One way 11 km, 7 miles
Hiking time 5 hours
High point 1420 meters, 4658 feet
Elevation gain 800 meters, 2624 feet
Map Kompass Wanderkarte 14

South of Salzburg and Berchtesgaden there is a dazzling glacier-carved lake rightly called Konigssee or King's Sea. With cliffs 800 meters high, the lake is as impressive as any fjord in Norway, New Zealand, or Alaska. A favorite tourist attraction is the boat ride from the town of Konigssee to the head of the lake, with a brief stop at St. Bartholoma Church, a charming structure with two onion-top steeples.

Impossible as it looks from the water, a trail really does climb from St. Bartholoma to the top of the cliff, providing superb views of the lake and the entire Watzmann Range. This is not a hike for young children or for adults who fear heights; and no one should take the hike on wet days when cliffs, ladders, wooden bridges, cables, and handholds are likely to be slippery.

When weather conditions are good, though, this hike is hard to beat for views of mountains and wildlife. We photographed a huge stag with gigantic antlers as he grazed near the Kuhrointhaus. And as we climbed up the trail, we were bombarded by pebbles loosened by some chamois — perhaps in anger at our presence. Early morning or late afternoon (with an overnight stop in a hut) are the best times to do this hike. Travel by bus or auto to Berchtesgaden. From there follow the signs to Konigssee, and buy a one-way boat ticket to St. Bartholoma, where the hike starts at 604 meters. In St. Bartholoma, walk toward the church and then uphill on a road going past a restaurant and several farm buildings. At ¾ km, turn right and walk a short distance downhill; you will find a trail signed "Watzmann Haus." For 4 km follow this rough, rocky, and steep trail, which climbs 600 vertical meters. The trail then enters the cliffs, crosses open space on a steeply tilted wooden trestle, switches back and forth like a whip, goes up ladders and onto narrow ledges—all with the lake in sight hundreds of meters below your boot tops. At 1400 meters the trail leaves the cliffs, enters the forest, and then becomes a road. The road climbs gently and leads to the Kuhrointhaus, a restaurant, where you will be ready to rest shaky legs, have a snack, and enjoy the view of 2713-meter-high Mittelspitze in the Watzmann Range. Standing out on a shoulder of the mountain is the Watzmann Haus.

From the restaurant there are several ways back to the starting point, and the most interesting is by way of the Grunstein Hutte (Gams Hutte). However, a storm was brewing, and we followed the trail marked "Schonau und Konigssee" because it was more direct. This is a broad, sometimes steep, and muddy path which ends in a maze of residential roads from which hikers must find their way back to the Konigssee parking lot.

Several other hikes are possible from the end of this huge glacial lake, which is an alpine phenomenon. Check the map for possibilities.

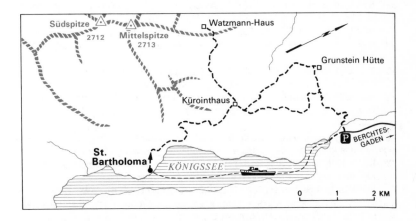

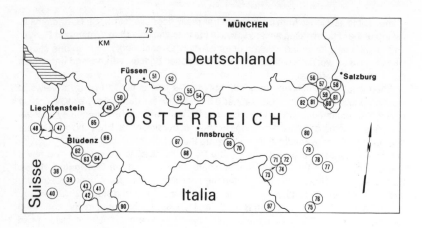

AUSTRIA - OSTERREICH

62 WINTERTAL (WINTER VALLEY)   Long day hike through alpine pastures to a high pass; return down a different valley. Near Schruns.

63 SAARBRUCKER HUTTE   Rough but beautiful trail leads to a mountain hotel under a glacier-clad peak; 1 day. Near Schruns.

64 WIESBADENER HUTTE   Loop trip starting beside a large reservoir, following a stream to a mountain hut with superb views; return down a different valley. Long day hike. Near Schruns.

65 KORBERSEE   Small lake reached in day hike through alpine fields. Near Lech.

66 DARMSTADTER HUTTE   Starting in forest, hike up a long valley to a hut overlooking a glacier; 1-2 days. Near St. Anton.

67 RINNENSEE   Small lake surrounded by glacier-carved mountains reached in strenuous day or easy 2-day hike. Near Innsbruck.

68 STUBAIER ALPEN GLACIER TRAVERSE   One-way hike passing four major glaciers. Long day or good overnight hike. Near Innsbruck.

69 SCHLEGEISKEES GLACIER   Hike around a large reservoir to a hut overlooking mountains and glaciers. Recommended as day trip, with longer alternative. Near Mayrhofen.

70 ZILLERTALER ALPEN GLACIER VIEW LOOP   Climb high above a reservoir surrounded by glacier-covered peaks; 1 day. Near Mayrhofen.

71 SLEEPING GLACIER   Valley walk, 6 km, then a steep climb to a mountain hotel beside a large glacier; 1 day, but recommended as overnight hike. Near Lienz and Mittersill.

72 FELBERTAUERNTUNNEL OVERPASS   A series of small lakes and great views highlight this long day hike across a mountain pass. Between Lienz and Mittersill.

73 NEUE REICHENBERGER HUTTE   Strenuous 2-day hike to a mountain lake and superb views, with alternate return route. Near Pragraten.

74 VENEDIGER GRUPPE (ESSENER-ROSTOCKER HUTTE)   Easy valley hike to magnificent glacier views, with strenuous alternate return route; 1 day. Near Pragraten.

75 LIENZER DOLOMITEN (KARLSBADER HUTTE)   Day hike to a mountain hut in the Austrian Dolomites. Near Lienz.

City of Lofer from Hundshorn trail (Hike No. 81)

76   EDERPLAN   Commanding views of the Dolomites and valley reached in strenuous day climb. Near Lienz.

77   ZIRMSEE   Steep trail hike beside a rushing torrent to an alpine lake; 1 day. Near Heiligenblut.

78   PASTERZENKEES GLACIER WALK   One of the shorter hikes (5 km) in the book, with a superb view of the glacier. From the Grossglockner Pass Highway.

79   STAUSEE MOOSERBODEN   Hike beside a reservoir surrounded by magnificent peaks; easy day hike to a viewpint or strenuous alternative hike completely circling the reservoir. Near Kaprun.

80   PINZGAUER SPAZIERGANG   Ridgetop traverse (24 km) from Zell Am See to Mittersill, with several shorter alternatives. Recommended for 2 days.

81   HUNDSHORN LOOP   Loop trip around a forested peak, with streams, a waterfall, and views; 1 day. Near Lofer.

82   LOFERER STEINBERGE (SCHMIDT-ZABIEROW HUTTE)   Steep climb to a mountain hut, with views of farms and villages; 1 day. Near Lofer.

62 WINTER TAL (WINTER VALLEY)

Round trip to Valzifenzerjoch 15 km, 9½ miles
Hiking time 6 hours
High point 2485 meters, 8151 feet
Elevation gain 1000 meters, 3280 feet
Map Unterwegs f & b 37

This hike takes you into an alpine valley with huge green meadows reddened in season by alpine rose, which is set off by large snowdrifts that last half the summer. On the rainy day in July we climbed up there, we had the valley and meadows all to ourselves. The hardy hiker can stretch this jaunt into a loop trip.

From Schruns, drive or take the Post Bus 14 km on highway 188 to the small resort town of Gargellen. When you have gone ½ km past the Schalbergbahn chair lift near a "Y" in the road, get off the bus or park your car in the small lot, elevation approximately 1475 meters. Walk the dirt service road on the right side of the Valzifenzbach (stream) for about ½ km to the point where the road crosses the stream. Stay on the right side and take the trail that parallels the water. It runs through forest most of the time and goes to the Madrisa Hutte, 1½ km. At the hut, cross the stream to the service road on the left side of the valley. At almost 4 km, you pass a waterworks where a trail crosses the stream, then climbs over Schlappinerjoch (pass) into Switzerland. Stay on the service road, which ends at a small building in a short distance.

From here the real trail starts, unmarked but plainly visible: it crosses the stream, which may be difficult in high water. The trail contours up the valley through a brilliant field of alpine rose, which begins to bloom in mid-July. At approximately 5½ km, the trail is a little tricky, so be alert. If you find yourself facing a stream crossing, you've gone too far; the trail crosses to the left side of the stream and is soon lost. Retrace your steps 100 meters to an obscure junction and you will most likely find the correct trail — it switchbacks up the right-hand hillside. If you cannot find this trail, climb up the slope and you will intersect it; the trail goes toward a cross that can be seen on the horizon.

At about 6 km, elevation 2221 meters, you reach a group of farmhouses where there are endless alpine meadows to explore, all with splendid views of the snowy slopes of

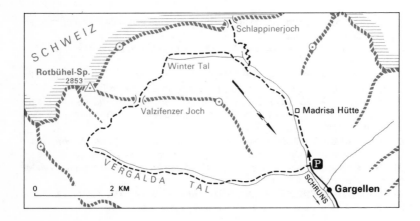

Farmhouses in Winter Tal (valley)

Rotbuhelspitze. For the loop trip, continue upward. Most of the way the trail is lost in a maze of cow paths, but we just kept aiming for the spot where the trail could be seen crossing Valzifenzerjoch, a pass at 2485 meters. This is as far as we were able to go. The weather had been poor when we started on this trail, and when we reached the pass we were engulfed in fog. It started to rain. Not wanting to hike a poorly marked trail under such conditions, we beat a hasty retreat. Although we did not make a loop by hiking the trail to its end, we know that the 16-km Vergalda Valley trail back to Gargellen is well used and at least partly on a service road. There should be no problem finding the way in clear weather.

63 SAARBRUCKER HUTTE

Round trip 12 km, 7½ miles
Hiking time 6 hours
High point 2538 meters, 8325 feet
Elevation gain 700 meters in, 150 meters out, 2788 feet
Map Kompass Wanderkarte 41 or Unterwegs f & b 37

The Silvretta region of western Austria is one of the finest hiking areas in the country. Good access roads lead to safe trails, huts are plentiful, and the mountains — the Silvrettahorn, Piz Buin, and others — are among the most beautiful in the Alps.

Take highway 188 past the city of Schruns, where Ernest Hemingway used to vacation with his family, and go toward Silvretta-Stausee Lake (reservoir). There is a hefty toll charge for using the road, but there is no way to avoid it. At Obervermuntwerk, at the upper end of the reservoir, you must choose a route: either walk up to the hut on the rather uninteresting service road (the sign said 2 hours, but we had our doubts), or ride to the Madlenerhaus (1968 meters), a mountain hotel located just below the concrete dam containing the Silvretta-Stausee, and take the trail. We preferred the trail even though it is longer and has several downgrades. In return for the extra effort, we found many wildflowers, lovely streams, and a greater variety of views.

The trail starts behind the hotel's most distant buildings. It makes a short descent, crosses a small stream, and, about 1 km farther, it starts up, first through a boulder field and then up a steep green hillside. At 2½ km, the trail crosses two streams; at 3½ km, it climbs over a promontory which offers the first views of the glacier-covered Grosse Seehorn and Grosse Litzner Mountains. Standing out boldly is the three-storied Saarbrucker Hutte.

The trail continues with ups and downs, and at 4½ km it crosses the Kromer Bach, a glacial stream which in springtime or after heavy rains may be difficult to ford. Some

Stream crossing

Grosse Seehorn. Saarbrucker Hutte on right side

snow patches may be found here. The trail joins a service road for about 100 meters and then climbs up steeply, avoiding the long switchbacks. At 6 km the trail and road reach the Saarbrucker Hutte, elevation 2538 meters, from which the views are splendid.

Experienced hikers may wish to go to other huts in the Silvretta region. However, the routes to many of these cross snowfields and include steep traverses where basic mountaineering equipment and skills are necessary.

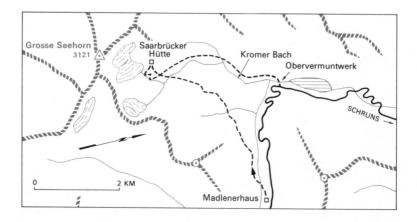

64 WIESBADENER HUTTE

Loop trip 13 km, 8 miles
Hiking time 5-6 hours
High point 2701 meters, 8862 feet
Elevation gain 665 meters, 2185 feet
Map Unterwegs f & b 37 or Kompass Wanderkarte 41

From the very beginning of this short hike the views are sensational; they get better the higher you go. In addition, elevation gain is only 400 meters; and by early summer the trip can be turned into a loop hike, with only 665 meters' elevation gain.

From Schruns (Hike No. 63), continue up the valley to the Silvretta-Stausee, elevation 2036 meters, where you can park. From the parking lot, contrary to the direction indicated on the trail sign, take the west side trail, crossing immediately over a high cement dam. At the end of the causeway, follow the lake, crossing several streams, and keep left at the various junctions. At about 3 km, you meet the east side trail; keep right. Ahead is the Ochsentaler Glacier with its many crevasses and long snowfields. At 4 km, the trail levels for a short distance while you parallel a rushing glacial stream. The meadows have a thick carpet of grass and during July many flowers grow here. A second broad glacier, the Vermunt, can now be seen at the end of the valley to the left of the Ochsentaler. The next 2½ km offer a pleasant, easy climb to the hut. On the way, two small glaciers become visible high up on the opposite side of the valley, and soon the several-storied hut can be seen. Since 1896 it has been a favorite spot to stop and have a drink or snack before going on.

If you have had enough, return the way you came; but if you want to prolong the pleasures, continue past the hut, take the left fork, and climb up to Radsattel. After a short but steep climb, you arrive at a fork. The trail to the right ends quickly at the snow-covered Tiroler Glacier. Take the trail marked with red and white paint stripes which heads straight uphill beside a small stream. After ½ km you reach a high, open, rocky alpine meadow. This is an ideal place to sit and soak in the view of splendid glaciers and peaks.

To complete the loop, continue across the rolling meadow and cross the Radsattel (2701 meters). The trail forks again at the saddle; the left fork continues to the top of

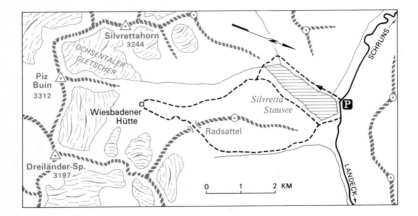

Bieltal (valley) from trail's end at Silvretta-Stausee

Hohes Rad (2934 meters), while the main trail crosses the pass and continues down into the Tirol.

The views on this side are pleasant, but not nearly as grand as the ones you have just seen. The trail goes down steeply for about 1 km (in July, when we hiked there, there were still snowfields), past a small but very blue lake, the Radsee, then down to a stream on the valley floor. In a gradual but steady descent, the route now follows the stream for 2½ km; at 3½ km from Radsattel, you swing around a bend and can see the Silvretta-Stausee.

65 KORBERSEE

Loop trip 12½ km, 7¾ miles
Hiking time 4 hours
High point 1800 meters, 5904 feet
Elevation gain 400 meters, 1312 feet
Map Kompass Wanderkarte 33

If the lake is your only destination, start from the village of Schroken. It is a short walk (1¼ hours) from there and even shorter if the ski lift is running. However, the lake was only one of many joys of our trip; we preferred starting from the town of Lech in order to enjoy alpine meadows and snowy peaks ending at the delightful mountain lake.

Lech, in the heart of the Arlberg region, is an expensive and very sophisticated resort. Hiking trails are poorly marked and there is no camping. Most of the mountains are strung like kites in the sky with ski lifts running up their faces and flanks; but there are still a few beautiful trails left for the hiker.

From the Lech Post Office, go north on road 198 toward Warth, 1¼ km, and find a small paved road, signed "Oberlech," climbing steeply uphill. Follow this road 400 meters to the first switchback and the trailhead, elevation 1500 meters, where you start the hike. (If you are driving, you can save considerable elevation by continuing on the paved road, following the signs to Gasthof Schlossle, at 1720 meters, where you can park and meet the trail.)

Back at the first switchback the unmarked trail starts as a narrow farm road, and at 1 km crosses under a ski lift. From there the trail becomes steep and at times muddy as it contours through alpine fields with occasional outcroppings of eroded limestone. At 2½ km, 1709 meters, you reach Auenfeld-Sattel (saddle), where you meet the trail coming from the Gasthof Schlossle. (This will be the return route.) From the saddle, follow a farm road downhill, passing through a barnyard and boulder-hopping the Bregenzer Ache (stream) twice. At 5 km from the start, elevation 1600 meters, leave the farm road and follow a well marked trail climbing to the Korbersee, a small mountain lake at 5½ km, elevation 1662 meters. On the right side of the lake is the Hotel Korbersee, while to the left are interesting rock formations.

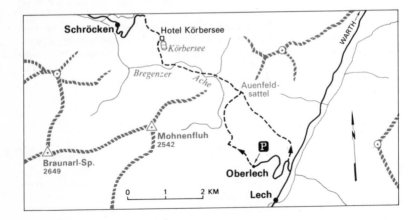

Farmhouse near Auenfeld-Sattel

For the return trip, retrace your steps to the Auenfeld-Sattel and take the trail headed south up a rounded knoll, climbing about 60 meters and passing through sumptuous fields of flowers. The flowers and views are the highlights of this hike. Then descend 60 meters, cross a stream in a narrow valley, and climb 80 meters to a paved road. Follow the road downhill past a gate to the Gasthof Schlossle at 2 km from Auenfeld-Sattel. There is no way to avoid the paved road for the final 2 km to Lech, but the views of mountain peaks, of lovely forest, and of Lech itself snuggled in the valley are worthwhile compensations.

151

66 DARMSTADTER HUTTE

Loop trip 20 km, 12½ miles
Hiking time 7 hours
High point 2384 meters, 7820 feet
Elevation gain 1098 meters, 3603 feet
Map Kompass Wanderkarte 33

This walk on a service road is as difficult as any trail hike. It has steep ascents, fords several small streams, and winds through a muddy pasture before reaching a mountain hut in an impressive glacial basin.

Route 138 from Bludenz to Innsbruck crosses a major pass, the Arlberg. Near the bottom of the pass lies St. Anton, the famous ski resort, where you will find good beer, wienerschnitzl, and Austrian atmosphere. Find a large parking lot near the Rendel ski lift. Below the lift is a wooden bridge, elevation 1286 meters. Cross the bridge and find a small sign indicating the Darmstadter Hutte. Follow the road as it switchbacks steeply across an open meadow and then heads into trees. Many short side roads take off as you climb up out of the valley, but stay with the main road. For 1 km the climb is steep, gaining 300 meters. Then you enter a forested side valley. One spur road goes down to a bridge and a small dam; but continue on the main road as it makes a slight descent before entering (at 2½ km) an open valley which is used for grazing. This is where the views begin in earnest.

The road follows the river bed up the valley, passing over several small streams. At 3½ km a spur road takes off to Tritsch Alpe and Jausenstation Moostal ski-hutte. It is possible to cross the river here and walk on a trail for 2 km, then recross the river on a footbridge and climb back to the road. After passing the spur, the road once again starts climbing. It gains approximately 300 meters through flowered meadows up to the Kartell Hutte (a farmhouse) at 1974 meters, 7 km from the starting point. As you continue up the road, the views become exciting. After the first switchbacks, the road straightens out, crosses the hillside to the end of the valley, and enters a delightful glacial basin. As the road rounds a curve in the valley, the Kuchel Spitze and Kuchen Spitze come into view. Lying between these two mountains is the idyllic Kuchel Glacier. At 10 km the road reaches the Darmstadter Hutte.

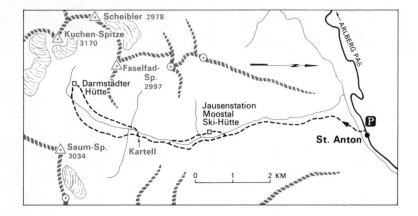

Moosbach (river) at Tritsch Alpe

The hut is located on a high green hill at 2384 meters, at the edge of a higher basin with excellent views of the Kuchen Glacier and Scheibler Mountain. From the Darmstadter Hutte, many trails and hiking routes go higher into the mountains, across glaciers, and over passes. See the recommended map for these.

67 RINNENSEE

Round trip 12 km, 7½ miles
Hiking time 5 hours
High point to Rinnensee 2650 meters, 8692 feet
Elevation gain to Rinnensee 900 meters, 2952 feet

High point to Rinnen-Spitz 3003 meters, 9850 feet
Elevation gain to Rinnen-Spitz 1253 meters, 4111 feet
Map Kompass Wanderkarte 83

The climb to the high mountain lake called the Rinnensee is delightful but strenuous. Views of the Stubaier Alpen are magnificent. The hardier hiker can reach the 3003-meter summit of the Rinnen-Spitz in one day.

From the Brenner Pass highway after Innsbruck travel up road 183 to Neustift. From the center of town a private jeep bus goes directly to the trailhead. If you are driving, follow the main Neustift street up the valley for 2 km until you reach an unmarked paved road headed uphill. Follow this road for 8 km to its end at a huge parking lot next to the Oberrisshutte, elevation 1750 meters, where trail 131 starts. After crossing a pasture, the trail switchbacks steeply over a wooded cliff, levels off, then climbs again to the Franz Senn Hutte, a large mountain hotel with a view of the Alpeiner Ferner (glacier), 2147 meters, approximately 3 km from the road. Walk to the front of the hut, cross a wooden bridge, then turn right, crossing a damp meadow. Then switchback up a cliff, with the help of a fixed steel cable, to a junction. Go left, climbing over 300 meters up a steep green slope to the top of a knoll and a grand viewpoint. The trail levels for a short distance, then climbs to the edge of the Rinnensee, through the huge boulders surrounding the lake, elevation 2650 meters. Even on the rainy day we were there we had a marvelous view of the Ruderhof Spitz and the glaciers radiating from numerous peaks.

On a clear day, the climb of the 3003-meter-high Rinnen-Spitz is well worth the extra effort. Go back down the trail a few meters to a junction and take the trail headed up the mountainside. The trail switchbacks up a steep hillside; then, with the aid of cables and some scrambling along the summit ridge, you reach the top. The views go to all points of the compass as well as down to the Lisenser Ferner (glacier).

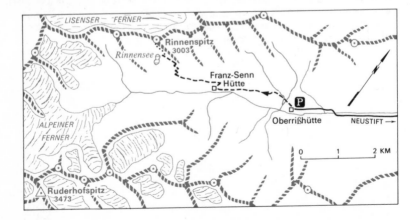

Signpost at the Franz Senn Hutte

68 STUBAIER ALPEN GLACIER TRAVERSE

One way 17 km, 10½ miles
Hiking time 8-10 hours
High point 2676 meters, 8777 feet
Elevation gain 1362 meters, 4467 feet
Map Kompass Wanderkarte 83

This traverse of a short section of the Stubaier Alps passes four major glaciers and offers views of many more. The trail is difficult, with long steep climbs and descents over boulder fields, talus slopes, and rock walls where you are protected by a cable. But the greatest hazard is spending too much time looking at the scenery and not enough time looking at where you are stepping.

Sulzenauferner (glacier) from Peiijoch

By Post Bus, train, or car, take the Brenner Pass autobahn from Innsbruck toward the Italian border. Turn off at Schonberg im Stubaital and go up the valley. On road 183 at Neustift, the road splits. Take the left fork toward Ranalt and continue to the ski resort at the end of the road. The trail starts here at 1750 meters. You can take the gondola lift to the first station and save 500 meters of climbing. If you prefer to walk, take trail 135, signed "Dresdner Hutte." The trail is in good condition, but it is a steady 3-km climb below the gondola cables ending at Dresdner Hutte, elevation 2250 meters, next to the gondola station.

From the top of the lift, go east, following signs to Sulzenauhutte on trail 102. The trail switchbacks up over a large boulder field to a rocky rib flanked by numerous needles so that from a distance it looks feathered. The trail makes a nerve-wracking ascent over the rib but you are aided by a cable and numerous built-in footholds and handholds. The trail then crosses a flat boulder field; at 1½ km it arrives at Peiijoch, 2676 meters, from which you can see the Sulzenauferner (glacier), with its broad flat expanse of blue ice splitting into deep crevasses near its snout.

Going down from the pass, the trail follows the thin rim of an old side moraine. Two lakes pop into view; Blaue Lacke is fed by snow melt, and a smaller grey pond is glacier-fed. At 2½ km the trail levels for a short distance before dropping to the Sulzenauhutte, 2191 meters, where drinks and post cards can be purchased. From here a tired hiker can return to the road by taking trail 136.

Otherwise, continue on trail 102 toward the Nurnberger Hutte. The trail climbs a short distance, then descends before climbing again steeply past several pretty lakes to a junction.

Stay on trail 102, climbing to the Niederl Pass up a steep rocky slope, then over a rock wall, again aided by a cable, to the pass, a narrow sharp ridge with a large cross, at 7 km, elevation 2627 meters. As it starts down, the trail is steep and difficult. However, cables offer extra support for shaky knees. At 8 km the trail arrives at Nurnberger Hutte, elevation 2280 meters, situated in the fourth glacial basin. The best views are found slightly above the hut.

The shortest route back to civilization, by way of Bsuchalm, is a long way. When you reach the road, you can take a bus back up the valley to a parked car, or down the valley to other hikes.

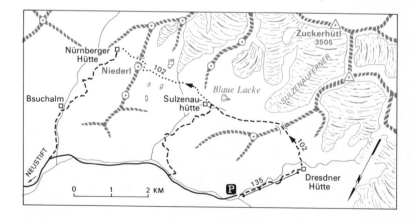

69 SCHLEGEISKEES GLACIER

Round trip 16 km, 10 miles
Hiking time 5 hours
High point 2295 meters, 7528 feet
Elevation gain 395 meters, 1296 feet
Map Kompass Wanderkarte 37

The Zillertal Alps south of Innsbruck offer a variety of hiking possibilities and abundant hut facilities, which make it possible to travel for several days with a light pack in a continually changing mountain environment. This hike brings you part of the way, the first day's segment.

From Innsbruck head east on the autobahn past Schwaz, then south on highway 169 to Mayrhofen. Continue on a toll road to the Schlegeisspeicher, a large reservoir, elevation 1782 meters. The way starts on a service road. A private taxi will take you up the road to the trailhead; or you can walk up the road (marked trail 502) as we and most of the other hikers did, and enjoy the ever-changing views around the lake. After 5 km the "traffic" ends. The trail begins at 1900 meters with seemingly endless switchbacks. But after each rocky hairpin turn, one is rewarded with views of permanent snowfields, icefalls, crevasses, and mountain landmarks which indicate the Austrian-Italian border. At approximately 8 km from the parking lot, elevation 2295 meters, the trail arrives at the Furtschagl Haus, a hut which hangs on a steep ridge. This is an excellent place to stretch out and enjoy the commanding views of the Schlegeiskees Glacier.

For hikers who have more time, trail 502 continues for another 35 km. The Wanderkarte map shows a difficult stretch on this trail, so we did not try it. Since then we have been told that while it is too difficult for a novice, an experienced hiker should be able to manage it. The problem is the high point, a 3081-meter pass between the Schonbichler Horn and the Furtschagl Spitz. If you have doubts, turn back.

Beyond the pass, it is up and down hiking between 2000 and 2700 meters until you descend to the Stilluppgrund Valley at 1500 meters. On the way huts are so well placed that they are never more than an easy day's hike apart. They offer plenty of food, a dry bunk, and Austrian good cheer.

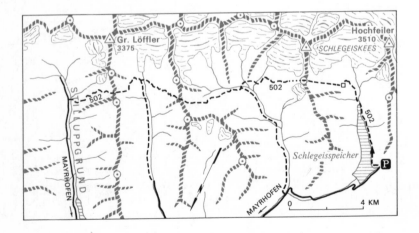

Schlegeiskees (glacier) from trail near the Furtschagl Haus

Schlegeisspeicher (reservoir)

70 ZILLERTALER ALPEN GLACIER VIEW LOOP

Loop trip 12 km, 7½ miles
Hiking time 5 hours
High point 2498 meters, 8196 feet
Elevation gain 798 meters, 2618 feet
Map Kompass Wanderkarte 37

This is a pleasant loop trip, mostly on easy trails, with excellent views of the glacier-covered mountains of the Zillertaler Alps high above a fjord-like reservoir. There is a small lake and a lively glacier-fed stream on which steep cascades and long waterfalls crash down.

From the Schlegeisspeicher Reservoir at 1800 meters (Hike No. 69), the trail takes off at a large advertisement for the Gasthaus Dominikushutte and a smaller sign for the Friesenberghaus on trail 532. Since the hut is supplied by pack horse, the trail is wide and gently graded. After a short climb the trail divides. Keep to the right; in ½ km the trail intersects a small service road. Continue straight ahead. Though rising steadily, the climb is never steep and often hardly noticeable. At 2 km the trail passes between two old farm buildings at Friesenberg Alm, 2036 meters, and rounds the corner of a hill; at 3 km the hut is visible. At 5½ km you arrive at the Friesenberg Haus, 2498 meters. Trail 526 to the Olperer Hutte takes off just below. Follow it down to the lake, which may well be covered with ice, then up the steep hill. This is the most difficult section of the trail. The loose talus and rocky cliffs give way after about 100 meters' elevation gain to a wide, nearly level trail which contours the hillside. The only difficulty here may be snowfields, but since this is a popular trail the path should be well beaten.

After a short descent, the trail arrives at Olperer Hutte, elevation 2389 meters. Unfortunately, views are limited at the hut. We recommend a 1-km side trip climbing 100 meters up the Weitwanderweg (trail) 502 for some of the best views of the trip.

To return to the valley from the hut, descend on trail 502, which is rough and rocky but wide. It makes the descent in a long series of well graded switchbacks. At 11 km, the trail arrives at the main lake road. Walk back 1 km along the lake to the starting point to complete the loop.

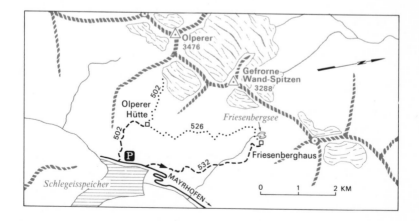

161

71 SLEEPING GLACIER

Round trip 24 km, 15 miles
Hiking time 10 hours
High point 2796 meters, 9171 feet
Elevation gain 1284 meters, 4212 feet
Map Kompass Wanderkarte 38

This steep hike takes you to a large hut located between two huge glaciers. The views are grandiose, particularly of the Grossglockner Mountain massif; and the hut is a splendid place to watch the sun rise on the Schlafenkees Glacier which, literally translated, means sleeping glacier. The first 6 km are on a toll road open to auto traffic for 2 hours early in the morning and 2 hours in the evening. The rest of the day it is swarming with walkers. The trail is steep, with stone stairways on a southeast slope. It can be very hot and dry in the morning sun.

By bus or auto, take highway 108 connecting Lienz and Mittersill. Leave the highway just before you reach the south end of the toll tunnel, and turn onto a road marked "Tauernhaus" with a sign advertising a chair lift. Go to a large parking lot and bus stop at the foot of the chair lift, elevation 1512 meters. Here's where you decide whether to drive and get on the trail quickly, or to walk the road and savor an ever-expanding view. During the first 2 km the road climbs through forest; then it levels out into alpine pastures—passing a quaint village, streams, and waterfalls, with glimpses of glaciers—until it ends at 6 km, elevation 1735 meters.

From there follow the way marked "Neue Prager Hutte." In a short distance cross a bridge over a torrent, then climb the steep green slope in a series of switchbacks. After you have climbed 600 meters, the views expand as the trail climbs above the snout of the glacier. At approximately 10 km from Tauernhaus you arrive at the Alte Prager Hutte, a small hut with refreshments. This is far enough for a day hike.

For those who wish to go on, the trail continues to climb across rubble fields and snow patches to the five-story Neue Prager Hutte, roughly 12 km from Tauernhaus, elevation 2796 meters, located between the broad Schlafenkees and the smaller Viltragenkees Glaciers. Tell the hutkeeper you want to stay overnight, then take in the glorious views.

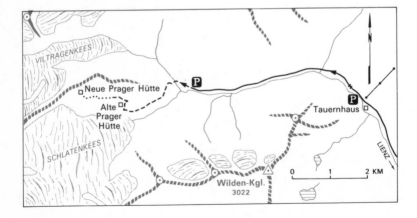

Hikers resting at the Alte Prager Hutte

You may be tempted to explore the smooth gentle slopes of the glacier; but unless you are equipped with ropes, ice axe, and crampons—and know how to use them—it would be inadvisable. Many crevasses are hidden underneath those innocent-looking snowfields.

72 FELBERTAUERNTUNNEL OVERPASS

One way 15 km, 9¼ miles
Hiking time (via normal route) 6½ hours
**   (via three lakes) 7½ hours**
High point 2563 meters, 8407 feet
Elevation gain 1200 meters, 3937 feet
Map Kompass Wanderkarte 38

While traffic roars through the Felbertauern tunnel, hikers can find scenic views, high alpine lakes, meadows, and fresh air on variety-filled trails over the tunnel, just off highway 108 connecting Lienz and Mittersill.

The hike may be started on the south or north side of the tunnel. We just happened to be on the south side. Follow the road directions for Hike No. 71. At the parking lot there is

Grauer See

a choice of walking up through pasturelands or taking the chair lift. Either way, the real decisions start at the top of the chair lift. From there two routes lead to the St. Poltener Hutte. The shorter route, called the Normalweg, is easy to follow, but it is badly scarred by power lines and towers. The first 3 km follow a service road, which contours around the hill into the next valley and continues up to the hut. This lower route must be taken in early summer when the upper route may be difficult due to snow or poor weather.

But given good conditions, the beautiful scenery is found on the upper trail, no. 512, by way of three lovely lakes. This route goes up the basin behind the lift, passing a T-bar. Climb up a steep hill to Gruner See (Green Lake), 2246 meters, where there is a small closed hut and a trail junction. Continue uphill. The top of the waterfall marks the position of the next lake, the Schwarzer See (Black Lake), 2344 meters. Passing the second lake, the trail follows a cascading river, climbs up yet another steep hill and over a loose talus slope to the third lake, Grauer See (Grey Lake), 2500 meters. Another short climb and the trail reaches Messling-Scharte (Gap), 2563 meters, at 6½ km. The outstanding views of the Venediger Gruppe are a great distraction as the trail contours down to another gap at 2498 meters. You climb steeply, with the aid of a metal cable, up the rocky side of a small knoll. After a short traverse over the top, you descend to the St. Poltener Hutte at 8½ km, 2481 meters.

From the top of the knoll above the hut you can see the first of a series of three lakes on the north side: the Tauernsee, the Langsee, and the Plattsee. Trail 917, heading toward Hintersee, passes right by the Plattsee at 10 km. The same trail drops again to cross the Tauernbach stream above a spectacular waterfall. Hikers, unable to follow the river bed, must climb a short distance before starting their descent at 12 km. After innumerable switchbacks, the trail arrives at a paved road at 15 km. Walk a short distance across a bridge to the parking area where there is bus service to Mittenwald.

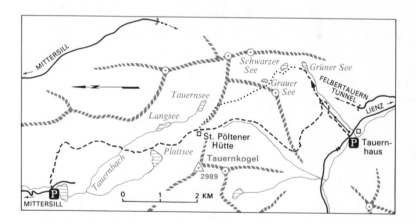

Bodensee and Neue Reichenberger Hutte

73 NEUE REICHENBERGER HUTTE

Round trip 16 km, 10 miles
Hiking time 8 hours
High point 2586 meters, 8482 feet
Elevation gain 1200 meters, 3936 feet
Map Kompass Wanderkarte 46

On this strenuous climb to a mountain hut next to a small alpine lake, the trail gains a lot of altitude, but the tantalizing glimpses of the Venediger Gruppe's massive glaciers make the effort more than worthwhile. Because it is a long and steep walk, some hikers turn this into a 2-day hike and stay overnight in the hut, returning the following day via the Daber Bach or walking down to St. Jacob in the next valley south.

By bus or car, travel highway 108 connecting Lienz and Mittersill to the town of Matrei, then follow signs to Pragraten. The views of the Grossglockner, elevation 3797 meters, and other high summits are framed by typical Tirolean villages. Continue past Pragraten to the last bus stop, at Hinterbichl, then go 1¾ km beyond to a large parking area and trailhead, elevation 1403 meters. Find the trail at the low end of the parking lot. It drops several meters to join a farm road and crosses a river; look for signs to the Neue Reichenberger Hutte. Stay on the farm road for 1¾ km to Pebell Alm, where there is a small mountain hut and restaurant, elevation 1513 meters. Pass in front of the hut, and immediately start climbing steeply up beside a waterfall. After gaining approximately 300 meters, the trail switches into a different watershed and continues its steep course, passing Sturmitzer Alm; then, at a lesser angle, it goes up to a high viewpoint at approximately 2100 meters, 4 km from the parking lot. For the next 2½ km the trail levels and, with more ups than downs, contours the hillside. Then comes a strenuous climb to a divide, with backviews of glacier-covered mountains. Neue Reichenberger Hutte at 2586 meters, surrounded by green meadows and jagged peaks, overlooks the Boden-see. It is approximately 8 km from the trailhead. If you have the energy, the climb up the green slopes of Bachlenken Kofl gives fine views of the glacier. After an overnight stay at the hut, you can take an interesting alternative return trip via the Dabertal Valley.

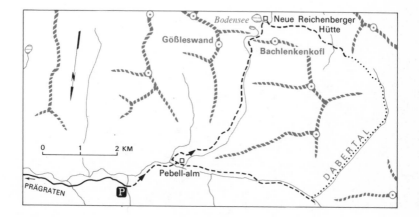

74 VENEDIGER GRUPPE (ESSENER-ROSTOCKER HUTTE)

Round trip to Essener-Rostocker Hutte 11 km, 7 miles
Hiking time 4 hours
High point 2208 meters, 7244 feet
Elevation gain 805 meters, 2642 feet
Map Kompass Wanderkarte 46

The Venediger Gruppe are high mountains covered with large, wide kees, the Austrian name for glaciers. Views and huts are accessible only by hiking. With just a couple of hours' effort, the hiker rises up out of the forest and lush meadowlands into fragile subarctic vegetation. Towering above are broad snowcapped peaks, many with elevations of 3400 meters or more, the sides of which are covered by unbroken snowfields veiling large glaciers, separated by sharp rock ridges. The open boulder-strewn slopes below the glaciers tempt the hiker to wander and explore for still better views, hidden peaks, or small lakes beside the glaciers.

One of the easiest means of access to the area is the Essener-Rostocker Hutte trail which takes off near the town of Pragraten. If the weather is good and legs and lungs are in shape, you can hut-hop from Essener-Rostocker Hutte to the Johannis Hutte. From there you will find several other fascinating glaciated valleys to explore. Then you can return to the main valley to within a couple of kilometers of your take-off point.

The trail starts from the upper end of the parking lot, elevation 1403 meters. (See Hike No. 73.) Head up the river toward Jausenstation and Stoan Alm following the Maurer-bach River for 1 km through lightly wooded forest to Stoan Alm at 1450 meters. Here the trail follows a gravel service road ½ km to its end at a small lift which is used to supply the Essener-Rostocker hut. The trail then climbs across a broad, steep, grassy hillside; at 3 km, the valley becomes suddenly steeper and the trail has to make several switchbacks. The climb is steady. At 4 km, 2068 meters, you pass a small decrepit farm hut; 700 meters farther, cross the river.

The Essener-Rostocker hut now can be seen perched on a high knoll above. At 5½ km, after another steep climb, you arrive at the hut, elevation 1208 meters, ready for a

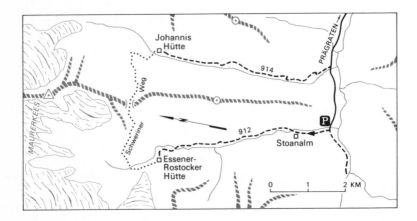

Trail crossing the Maurerbach (river)

cool drink. Beyond the hut there are many interesting routes with breathtaking views. You can continue to the end of the valley to see the sweeping Maurerkees. A side trip just after you cross the first bridge from the hut goes to two glacier lakes; the upper lake is at the snout of the Malhamkees Glacier. This area has many shiny micaceous metamorphic rocks rich in small reddish-brown garnets.

A rough but marked route to Johannis Hutte takes off from the Essener-Rostocker Hutte. The trail, called the Schweriner Weg, crosses a 2800-meter-high pass, and should be taken only in late summer when the way is free of snow and the weather is clear.

75 LIENZER DOLOMITEN (KARLSBADER HUTTE)

Round trip 7 km, 4¼ miles
Hiking time 3½ hours
High point 2260 meters, 7415 feet
Elevation gain 640 meters, 2100 feet
Map Kompass Wanderkarte 47

The Lienzer Dolomiten group offer an enchanting area for hiking and roaming. Above green meadowlands rise high, sharp peaks popular among the international climbing community. Consequently, there are well worn trails leading to the base of every mountain and up every pass. The area is easily accessible for those traveling by car; but drivers should be warned that toll roads are numerous and expensive.

The Karlsbader Hutte is on the shores of the Laserzsee; its lovely views of mountains, lakes, and the valley below make it extremely popular. From Lienz take the bus or drive south toward Amlach and Tristach. There is a confusion of roads to be sorted out, but one must go about 1 km east after Tristach and take the second turn to the right. The road is paved. A sign near the bus stop indicates the way to the Karlsbader Hutte trail. The road goes on past a turnoff to a campground and Tristacher See. At 3¼ km the road is barred by a gate and a toll must be paid. At about 7½ km, the road ends at a parking lot and trailhead, elevation 1627 meters.

Several minutes' walk on a gravel road brings you to the Lienzer Dolomiten Hutte. About ½ km farther is a trail junction with two possible routes to the Karlsbader hut. Follow the narrow service road on the right, because the left trail is a climbers' route which crosses two peaks before returning to civilization. Approximately 1½ km past Insteil-Alm, 1669 meters, the way is now close to a small stream which is notable because the water comes out from under the gravel of the river bed. Above is a dry channel used by the river during flood times. At this point you may continue up the road or take the fussweg (footpath), which is more direct and steeper, climbing steadily until it reaches the hut and Laserzsee at 3½ km, 2260 meters.

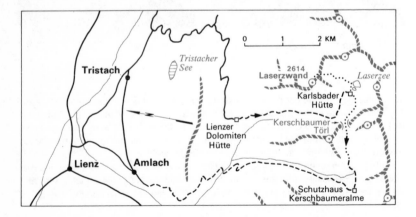

Lienzer Dolomiten

From the hut there are several interesting trips to mountain saddles which offer views into distant valleys. By walking 1 km on the trail toward Schutzhaus Kerschbaumer-Alm, you will reach Kerschbaumer Torl Pass and a broad open view of Kerschbaumer-Alm. If you have not left a car on the road below, you may wish to continue over the pass for an enjoyable stroll into the valley. From Amlach a bus will bring you back to Lienz.

76 EDERPLAN

Round trip 12 km, 7½ miles
Hiking time 5 hours
High point 2061 meters, 6760 feet
Elevation gain 500 meters, 1640 feet
Map Kompass Wanderkarte 47

Summit of the Ederplan

From the city of Lienz you can see a dome-shaped mountain topped with a huge cross. This is the Ederplan. A number of trails lead to the top: one goes from Gortschach at 760 meters, and another from Iselsberg at 1050 meters. We were feeling lazy, so we chose the latter, the easier climb.

From Lienz, travel north on highway 107 (by bus or car) to Iselsberg. On a sharp switchback, opposite the Gasthof Dolomitenblick and next to a bus stop, take the road marked "Stronach," elevation 1050 meters. This road can be driven 1¼ km to Stronach, a

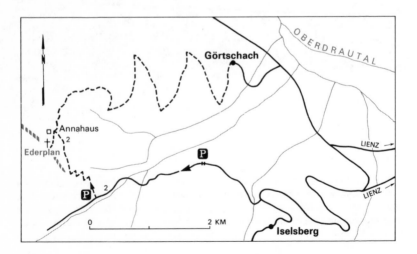

Valley near Lienz from side of Ederplan

tiny cluster of farmhouses where there is a tollgate, 1105 meters. If the gatekeeper is present, pay the toll and drive another 2 km to the trailhead. Otherwise, walk up the road.

The way is well marked with signs indicating Ederplan and Anna Schultz Haus, and the number 2, the trail number, painted on rocks and trees. At 2 km (3¼ km from Iselsberg), there is a well marked trailhead. The climb starts out steeply, switchbacking through a logging clearing and then entering a forest, passing Eder Alp, a small barn with a mammoth view, at 1614 meters. The way continues steeply up and at approximately 1800 meters the grade eases. The trail contours around the mountain to Anna Schultz Haus, a 90-year-old mountain hut. A plaque says it was a gift made in 1887 to the Austrian Touring Club from the artist Franz Van Detregger. The building is now used as a mountain restaurant.

From the restaurant it is only a short distance to the Ederplan, 2061 meters, approximately 6 km from Iselsberg. On top are the giant cross, surrounded by fields of blueberries, and fabulous views of the Oberdrautal Valley and the city of Lienz. The rugged peaks of the Dolomites lie to the south; and to the north the rocky peak of Petzeck and the glacier-clad mountains of the Grossglockner Gruppe can be seen.

77 ZIRMSEE

Round trip 14 km, 9 miles
Hiking time 7 hours
High point 2495 meters, 8183 feet
Elevation gain 700 meters, 2296 feet
Map Kompass Wanderkarte 50

Waterfalls and rushing torrents make this hike to an alpine lake very noisy, if pleasing. Take a bus or drive to Heiligenblut on highway 107, located on the south side of the famous Grossglockner-Hochalpenstrassen (road). From Heiligenblut go uphill on 107 to the first switchback (there is a bus stop), approximately 2 km above the village, and follow a narrow paved road that goes straight ahead a scant ½ km as it literally dips under a barn and comes to a junction. This is the starting point at 1514 meters. Eventually, it may be possible to drive farther up this road; but when we were there, construction for a water project was in progress.

Follow a dirt road uphill. Whenever the road switchbacks, hikers will find a good trail shortcutting it. Follow the road up the valley, crossing the stream at 1½ km, and reach the Alter Pocher Hutte at 3 km, elevation 1807 meters. From the hut the trail stays on the left side of the valley, although some maps show it on the right, climbing steadily—always within the sound of the torrent and often in sight of waterfalls. For a short distance the trail competes with a small stream for the right of way. When the stream wins, take to the bank. At 4 km cross a torrent on a flimsy bridge. From there the trail climbs around cliffs and leaves the valley for the climb to the lake.

We hiked this trail in bad weather on the first day of August. There had just been several stormy days and the peaks were covered with fresh snow down to the 2000-meter level; so it was no surprise when a snowstorm hit us as we were passing around the cliffs. The trail became slippery, the wind intense. We turned back. We were obliged to take the word of the campground manager that the 2495-meter-high Zirmsee is a lovely little lake, surrounded by green alpine meadows topped by craggy peaks.

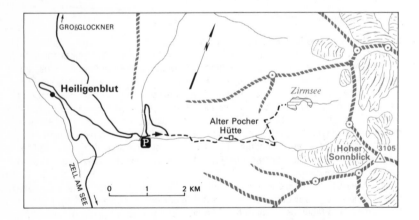

Trail to Zirmsee

78 PASTERZENKEES GLACIER WALK

Round trip 5 km, 3 miles
Hiking time 2 hours
High point 2600 meters, 8528 feet
Elevation gain 231 meters, 758 feet
Map Kompass Wanderkarte 39 or 50

This short trail will take you close to the snout of a glacier in the Grossglockner massif. Along the way are views of the Grossglockner, which at 3770 meters (12,369 feet) is the highest summit in Austria. Best of all, this trail lets you observe a glacier at work. You will note how the higher reaches of the glacier are white where the snow accumulates to great depths and is eventually compressed into ice. You will see the area where the downward flow is rapid (as much as 10 centimeters, roughly 4 inches, per day), like water flowing over a rough river bed and causing ripples on the surface. And you will see how, as the glacier bends, its surface cracks, causing crevasses. Eventually, at the snout, the lighter snow is melted away, leaving nothing but solid ice, which is very blue in certain lights.

The trail is wide enough to accommodate many people. Because falling rock is a danger, the trail is closed during rainstorms and thawing periods. As is the case on many other trails in this region, hikers should stop when the trail crosses a glacier unless they are experienced glacier travelers.

Take the Grossglockner-Hochalpenstrassen (highway 107) toll road between Zell Am See and Lienz over the 2575-meter-high Hochtor Pass. On the south side of the pass, drive the scenic glacier view road to its end at a parking garage next to a hotel, restaurant, and souvenir shop. The trail starts as a passageway at the far end of the garage and then enters a short tunnel. The trail, blasted from slabs of glacier-scoured rock, is wide and smooth, built for the small trucks that supply the mountain huts. At 1¼ km you pass above Hofmanns Hutte, and then at 2½ km from the garage reach the road's end at a cascade of water, elevation 2600 meters. From here a good trail continues another 300 meters, but this is the beginning of a climbers' route across the

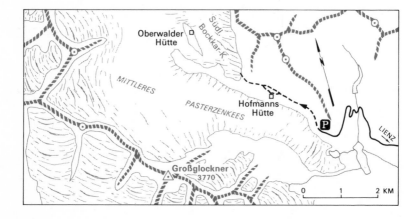

Hofmanns Hutte and Pasterzenkees (glacier)

glacier to the Oberwalder Hutte. As noted earlier, unless you are experienced in glacier travel, stop here. This is a perfect place to study the glacier. Walk 200 meters uphill, to the snout of the Sudl. Bockkarkees Glacier. Note the rock- and mud-covered ice, and the deep striations on bare rocks caused by the moving sea of ice.

79 STAUSEE MOOSERBODEN

**Round trip to knoll 11 km, 7 miles
Hiking time 3½ hours
High point 2100 meters, 6888 feet
Elevation gain 100 meters, 328 feet**

**Loop trip 10 km, 6¼ miles
Hiking time 6 hours
High point 2550 meters, 8364 feet
Elevation gain 600 meters, 1968 feet
Map Kompass Wanderkarte 39**

Ptarmigan

On the day we hiked to the Stausee Mooserboden reservoir we saw a herd of chamois and a mother ptarmigan with chicks. This hike can be either a round trip to an inspiring viewpoint or, for the experienced mountain hiker who is used to hiking on snow, a loop trip completely around the big reservoir. Either way, the trip should not be undertaken before mid-July, when the steep snow slopes bordering the trail on the southeast side of the lake have diminished. You also need to be careful on hot days when glacier-fed streams are flooding. Some torrents can become difficult to ford.

Getting to the trail is almost as exciting as the hike. From Kaprun, located southwest of Zell Am See, go approximately 8 km by bus or car up Kapruner Tal (valley) to the end of the public road. To avoid the hordes of tourists, it is best to arrive early. At the parking lot, catch a Post Bus which travels a one-way road through a series of tunnels; at road's end, transfer to an inclined railroad; and then at railroad's end, board another bus which

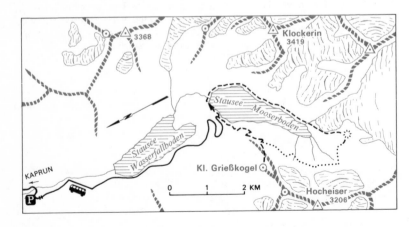

Stausee Mooserboden

goes through another series of tunnels, climbing past Stausee Wasserfallboden to the top of the dam impounding Stausee Mooserboden, elevation 2036 meters.

After all that public transport, now go by foot. Hike across the 1-km-long dam. On the far side follow the very obvious trail above the lakeshore, climbing slightly over cliffs then descending a ledge protected with handrails. After that the trail remains level, and you boulder-hop several wild glacial streams whose source can be found a few hundred meters higher. At 4 km you reach the head of the lake and cross a bridge over a large stream. The trail then climbs towards a high green knoll, elevation approximately 2100 meters. It's a wonderful place to sit and contemplate the grandeur of nature in contrast to the works of man.

To continue the loop, follow the trail up the side valley until you reach a junction. Take the unsigned right fork. The trail is faint but visible as it crosses high open meadows. Above, it goes through rocky slopes and is even fainter, following cairns and paint marks. The direction is clear, however, and the attentive hiker should have no problem. The trail climbs over talus slopes, level snowfields, and moraines to 2550 meters, then traverses a shelf high above the lake between waterfalls below and small glaciers above.

At 8½ km, the route climbs over a steep cliff to a large cairn at the end of a green shelf. Following the paint marks, walk across this shelf, heading slightly downhill, until you meet a large trail going up to Kleine Griesskogel. Head downhill on this trail to the starting point.

80 PINZGAUER SPAZIERGANG

One way 32 km, 20 miles
Hiking time 2 days
High point 2000 meters, 6560 feet
Elevation gain 800 meters, 2624 feet
Elevation loss 1900 meters, 6235 feet
Map Kompass Wanderkarte 30 and 38

This is one of the longest and most interesting ridge hikes in the Alps. You walk 32 km from Zell Am See to Mittersill, with views to the north of the barren crags along the German-Austrian border, and views to the south of the Glockner massif's huge glaciers. The ridge follows the fringe of the timberline. Although it's a long walk, you gain the initial elevation by taking a cable car; from then on the trail contours around the high points and is mostly level. Since there are numerous alternate trails back down to the valley, you can leave the high country whenever you wish for overnight stays.

From the center of Zell Am See catch a bus to the Schmittenhohebahn (cable car). Buy a one-way ticket and ascend to 1865 meters. From there the trail starts by steeply descending to a saddle with ski lifts, elevation 1700 meters. Follow the ski trail west along the ridgetop, but just before reaching the top of the lift (1800 meters), take the trail leading to the left. It now traverses the hillside with only very minor ups and downs. At 4 km you pass a ski hut and then climb to an elevation of 1900 meters. At 7 km there is a trail down to Steindorf, where transportation and lodging can be found. At 8 km the trail climbs to a 2000-meter saddle; at 10 km a second trail goes down to Steindorf. Between 11 and 13 km the trail contours steep slopes under the Hochkogel. At 14 and 17 km there are trails down to Uttendorf. At 19 km the trail crosses below the Pihappenkogel. The trail drops a little, then climbs to a 2000-meter saddle which is at 23 km; from there it descends and reaches the Burglhutte at 24 km. A service road will take you back to the valley bottom either at Stuhlfelden or Mittersill. From there take a bus back to Zell Am See.

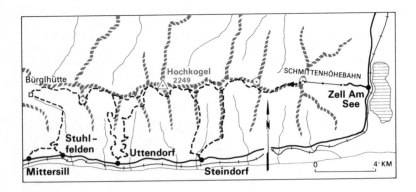

Glockner massif from Pinzgauer Speziergang trail

81 HUNDSHORN LOOP

Loop trip 14 km, 9 miles
Hiking time 6 hours
High point 1450 meters, 4756 feet
Elevation gain 750 meters, 2460 feet
Map Kompass Wanderkarte 13

Waterfall from Kematstein-Alm

If you are looking for a 360-degree view of magnificent peaks, valleys, villages, farms, and forests—with an 80-meter-high waterfall thrown in for good measure—then the loop trip around the 1703-meter-high Hundshorn is for you.

From the junction of highways 312 and 311 near the city of Lofer, travel a stone's throw south on 311 and turn east on a road marked "Scheffsnother-u-Hunds-Alm." Cross a concrete bridge and from the maze of narrow roads choose the one that goes left. By the water trough in the village of Scheffsnother turn right, then left. If you can find them, follow the signs indicating Knappenftadl, a restaurant which can be seen on the hillside above. When you get to the restaurant, 3 km from the highway, the elevation is 800 meters. The trail starts here.

The trail is marked with a lengthy sign which lists, among other names, "Joching-Alm, Scheffsnother, Hunds-Alm." Starting as a service road, the trail makes a short switchback around a gravel pit, then leaves the road and climbs steeply to the right. Be careful at this point because the trail is unmarked. It is extremely steep and climbs to the 1226-meter-high Kematstein-Alm in a very tiring kilometer. From there the trail levels off and contours around a small but deep valley at the head of which you can see and hear a waterfall that plunges about 80 meters. At 1¾ km you reach a junction with the Joching-Alm trail, which will later be your return route. Keep to the right, first on the level, then climbing in view of the waterfall. Your reward for taking steep switchbacks above the waterfall will be a beautiful glade with heather, trees, and a little bubbling brook which is obviously the source of the waterfall. The trail then crosses the brook and climbs up to Scheffsnother-Alm, which is at 1354 meters. Crossing the alm (pasture), the trail is once again hard to find; head for the highest point in the alm where the trail crosses over a saddle at 1450 meters. From the saddle, you can take a side trail for a long kilometer (and 1½ extra hours for the round trip) to the top of 1703-meter-high Hundshorn, where you will enjoy unlimited views.

Back at the saddle, the trail, scratched from a steep hillside, continues north; it drops to Hunds-Alm and then down to a 1323-meter-high saddle and a five-way trail junction. From the junction take the trail marked "Joching-Alm." It climbs a little, then drops as it contours under the steep wooded hillside below the Hundshorn. The Joching-Alm is reached at about 9½ km, elevation 1300 meters. Go to the lowest point and take the right-hand trail, which drops in a series of short switchbacks into a steep gully. There, near Kematstein-Alm, the trail joins the first trail you came up. Take that trail and hike back to the trailhead, which is at the Knappenftadl restaurant.

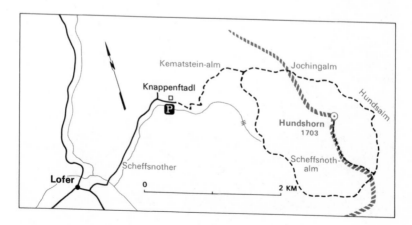

Soldanelles melting through last winter's snow

82 LOFERER STEINBERGE (SCHMIDT-ZABIEROW HUTTE)

Round trip 9 km, 5½ miles
Hiking time 6 hours
High point 1996 meters, 6547 feet
Elevation gain 1196 meters, 3923 feet
Map Kompass Wanderkarte 13

The stone mountains of Loferer are well named. They rise out of timber-covered slopes and dominate the village. All trails into the area are very steep; they gain considerable elevation in a relatively short distance. Above the stone shoulders, however, the going is easier and the hiker is free to wander and explore in several directions along well marked routes. Wildflowers are abundant in lower meadows, giving way, at higher elevations, to the small hardier species found in rocks and small crags.

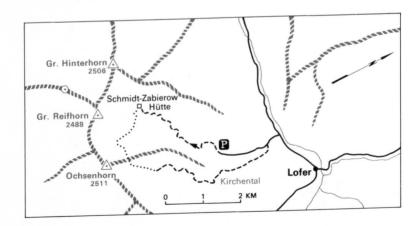

Schmide-Zabierow Hutte

From Lofer the trail can be reached by bus or car. Take highway 311 or 312 and at the junction of the two roads just south of town, take 312 toward Innsbruck. At 1¼ km, there is a road to the left which has no name, but it is marked by a direction sign to the Schmidt-Zabierow Hutte and a bus stop. Walk or drive 1¾ km up the paved road. Keep left and avoid the army camp. The road ends at a small parking lot, elevation 880 meters. The trail takes off on what appears to be an old road. Pass to the right of a small shack, then follow the signs toward Schmidt-Zabierow Hutte and the red paint dots on trail 601. The trail stays on the valley floor until it reaches cliffs at the valley's end, marking the start of the climb, then takes a turn to the left and begins a long series of switchbacks. First it goes up through forest, where an occasional chamois may be seen, then the trees give way to meadows, and the trail goes up over a series of large steps. The map names three: Unter, Mittleres, and Oberes Tret (lower, middle, and upper step); but when you are hiking up, it seems more like thirty. Towards the top the vegetation is replaced by weathered limestone. The trail weaves its way through the rocky slabs then up a small knoll to the hut, elevation 1966 meters, located in a large cirque.

Weather and time permitting, let ambition dictate your route. You have several choices. If you want to return by the same trail, wander on any of the marked routes through the cirques. But instead, consider taking route 613 to Ochsenhorn and Kirchental. This steep, rocky, and slippery trail is difficult but full of interest. Follow the double red stripes over several ridgetops and past two trail junctions. The third junction is the Ochsenhorn trail now marked with one red paint stripe. A bit of easy scrambling down the steep slope will take you to the valley head. Farther down there is a large church, which probably gave Kirchental Valley its name. Just past the church a trail leads back to Lofer.

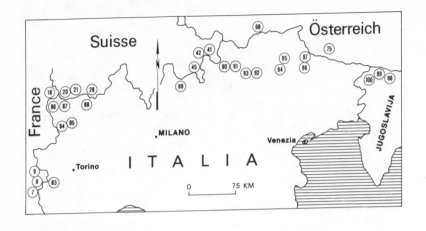

Brenta Dolomites (Hike No. 92)

ITALY - ITALIA

18   LE TOUR DU MONT BLANC (TMB)   Loop trip around Mont Blanc, passing through a corner of France and Switzerland; 10 days, 160 km.

83   TOUR AROUND MONT VISO   Loop trip around Mont Viso on the French-Italian border, with valleys, forests, streams, lakes, and flowers; 3 days. Reached from Torino in Italy or Guillestre in France.

84   RIFUGIO VITTORIO EMANUELE, GRAN PARADISO NATIONAL PARK   Day climb on a steep trail to a mountain hut located below Monte Gran Paradiso. Near Aosta.

85   GRAN PARADISO LAKES, GRAN PARADISO NATIONAL PARK   A group of mountain lakes reached in 2-day hike. Near Aosta.

86   MONTE BIANCO VIEW   Ridge walk with superb views of Mont Blanc's south side; 1 day. Near Courmayeur.

87   GRAND COL FERRET   Climb over alpine meadows to a view of Mont Dolent and other peaks of the Mont Blanc massif; 1 day. Near Courmayeur.

88   MONTE CERVINO   Flower-covered meadows on the Italian side of the Matterhorn highlight this day hike. Near Aosta.

89   SENTIERO ROMA   Day hikes or 3-day loop on a rugged trail in the Bernina Alps. Near Lake Como.

90   HINTER-SCHONECK, STELVIO NATIONAL PARK   Long, steep day climb to a 3128-meter peak, with grand views of the park. Near Glurns.

91   RIFUGIO G. PAYER, STELVIO NATIONAL PARK   Long, steep, 2-day climb to a hut located on a narrow ridge high on Monte Ortles. Near Glurns.

92   DOLOMITI DI BRENTA   From Madonna di Campiglio, southwest of Bozon, 1-day or week-long hike on spectacular trails among towering cliffs.

93   VAL NAMBINO LAKES LOOP   Day hike to alpine meadows, streams, lakes, and views of the Brenta Dolomites. Starts at Madonna di Campiglio.

94   SELLA DOLOMITES   After a bus ride to a mountain pass, a short day hike back to the starting point, crossing under towering cliffs. Views of mountain climbers. Near Corvara.

95   PUEZ DOLOMITES   Hike on a high plateau with fascinating rock formations; 1 day or longer. Near Corvara.

96   SEXTENER DOLOMITES   Day hike on a spectacular trail that wanders under towering pinnacles, is blasted across cliffs, and goes up ladders. Near Cortina.

97   TRE CIME   Loop hike among the cliffs and peaks of the Sextener Dolomites; 1 day or longer. Near Cortina.

YUGOSLAVIA - JUGOSLAVIJA

98   LAKE BLED   Short walk from the city of Bled for views of a famous lake in the northwest mountains of Yugoslavia.

99   MOUNT TRIGLAV (DOM STANICA), MOUNT TRIGLAV NATIONAL PARK   The beautiful peaks of the Julian Alps are the backdrop of this hike; 2-3 days. Near Mojstrana.

100   LEPA KOMNA   Hike in the Julian Alps on pleasant forest and meadow trails, past relics of World War I; 1-2 days. Near Bovec.

83 THE TOUR AROUND MONT VISO

Round trip approximately 30 km, about 19 miles
Hiking time 2-3 days
High point 2914 meters, 9558 feet
Elevation gain 2000 meters, 6560 feet
Maps Michelin No. 77; D&R Massifs du Queyras & Haute Ubaye

When you are in good shape and ready to tackle long distances, try this 2-3 days' delight around Mont Viso. Although the hike is mostly in Italy, and its atmosphere is Italian, you can approach it from the French town of Abries by driving up route 547 to the Belvedere du Viso. In Italy, drive up from the town of Crissolo to the 2115-meter-high Plan del Re hut and leave your car there.

Farmhouse in Vallanta Valley

The beauty of this tour lies in its scenic variety—rich valleys and forests, flowing streams and clear lakes, flowers in meadows and in high pastures, forest and rock trails, and several passes with views of Mont Viso, 3841 meters high, and hundreds of peaks in the Piedmont Alps and the national park nearby. The four huts along the way, although noisy with climbers and hikers, serve hot meals and provide bunk beds.

From the Plan del Re Albergo (a mountain hotel), cross over the source of the Po River and climb well defined switchbacks to the Refuge Sella, a trip of about 2½ hours. The trail beyond the albergo is remarkably well maintained and clearly marked with dashes of red-orange paint, old cigarette wrappers, and tin cans left behind prominent rocks. We are sorry to mention such details; our hope is that this already splendid hike will be made more beautiful once this pollution problem is solved. At the Passo Gallarino, keep to the right fork of the trail, following the marks. Shortly thereafter cross the Passo S. Chiaffredo and then follow the stream over the rough rock trail into the valley. As you approach the forest there are some excellent sites for tenting.

The second day the vegetation and views change dramatically as you climb up the Vallante Valley, past shepherds' huts, troops of cows and sheep, and the Refuge Gagliardone to the steep Col de Vallante. Many marmots have tunneled through the hills, and edelweiss, bluebells, myosotis, margaritas and many other kinds of flowers can be found. The steep trail passes to the left of the refuge and its lake and finally crosses into France at the Col de Vallante. Here you may find a lot of snow; you will want to exert extreme care on these patches, particularly if you reach them early in the morning when they may not have started to thaw.

The French Baillif-Viso refuge is at 2455 meters and was built in 1976. From Easter to September 15, hot meals are served by the hutkeeper. We pitched our tent about 20 minutes from the refuge, and as the sun went down we enjoyed French views of Mont Viso. The next day we climbed in 2½ hours back to Italy through the Col de la Traversette and down to Plan del Re.

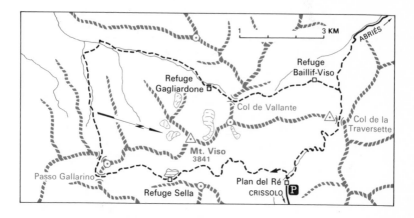

84 RIFUGIO VITTORIO EMANUELE
Gran Paradiso National Park

Round trip 8 km, 5 miles
Hiking time 5 hours
High point 2732 meters, 8961 feet
Elevation gain 772 meters, 2532 feet
Map Carta Turistica Gran Paradiso-Valle d'Aosta 86

This hike takes you to a refuge high on the side of Gran Paradiso Mountain. You explore meadows and search for the elusive ibex and chamois. Do not expect solitude, however. The Gran Paradiso is one of the most popular attractions in the Italian national parks. The entire area was once the private hunting preserve of Italian royalty. Although the mountain ibex was hunted into extinction elsewhere in Europe, about 100 animals survived in this preserve. Since 1911, ibex from the park have been sent to many nature reserves throughout the Alps. There are now somewhere between 7000 and 10,000 animals.

The main entry to the park, the Val Savaranche, is located a few kilometers west of Aosta. As far as we know, public transportation up the valley is erratic, although the intention is there: one is encouraged by the bus stop signs. If you don't have a car, you can try to hail a ride from a passing Alfa or Ferrari on its way up to Paradise Mountain from Rome or Florence.

The Gran Paradiso hike starts at Pont Breuil, 1960 meters, at a large road-end parking lot. The trail is poorly marked but well defined by the constant international traffic of hikers and climbers. From the lot cross the Savara River on a bridge, hike upriver 1 km, and cross a stream to a trail junction. Go left. In a few meters the trail starts a series of short switchbacks, climbing steeply first in forest then through open slopes, 300 meters in 1½ km. Although the switchbacks lengthen, the trail keeps going steadily upward to the two-story Refugio Vittorio Emanuele at 4 km, elevation 2732 meters.

From the refuge there is a superb view of ice- and snow-covered Mount Ciaforon and the gently sloping Montcorve Glacier; but to see the summit of the Gran Paradiso, one must go higher. After a dinner of pasta, goat cheese, and chianti, and a good night's

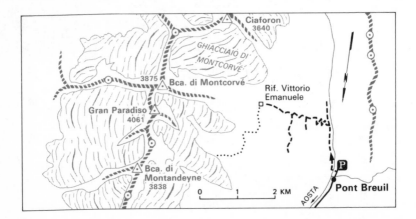

Pont Breuil and trail to Rifugio Vittorio Emanuele

sleep, try to get up early. That's when you can best pick out the peaks and the animals. Three unmarked trails contour north. The first, a few hundred feet above timberline, goes only a short distance. The second, a seldom used but well built trail, goes for 1 km to the edge of a cliff. From there a sketchy path contours around a steep hillside. The third trail is a faint path from the refuge through a large rockslide to glacier-scoured rock and moraine. The second and third trails offer good chances to see the animals and your first views toward the summit of the Gran Paradiso.

To return to Pont Breuil, retrace your steps from the refuge.

85 GRAN PARADISO LAKES
Gran Paradiso National Park

Round trip 20 km, 12½ miles
Hiking time 2 days
High point 2700 meters, 8856 feet
Elevation gain 740 meters, 2428 feet
Map Carta Turistica 86 Gran Paradiso-Valle d'Aosta (Attention: Some trails
marked on this map do not exist)

On this trip into the lake country called the Piani del Rosett you can wander around a high green plateau full of lakes, peaks, snowfields, and glaciers. In season, the plateau abounds with birds and wildflowers and there is even the elusive edelweiss. Because of the distances and the many lakes, this hike is best taken in 2 days; but that is relatively easy since there are two hotels about 9 km out.

The plateau can be reached from two directions: up the Orco River Valley, 66 km from the town of Irvea, or from France through the Mont Blanc tunnel and then up the Val Savaranche from near Aosta. A road that has been under construction for many years will eventually connect the two valleys and add many more people to the already popular area.

The trail starts at elevation 1900 meters, from the hamlet of Pont Breuil at the end of the road going up the Val Savaranche. From the parking lot, walk back down the road about 300 meters and just before crossing a bridge, find an unmarked trail leading up the left (south) side of a stream. At first the grade is easy, but the trail soon becomes a series of steep short switchbacks as it climbs 350 meters in less than 1 km.

Once you reach the crest of the hill, the trail levels out and at 2 km you enter a large flat valley. To avoid marshy areas, the trail skirts the edge of the valley and eventually joins the unfinished road. At 9 km you reach the first of two mountain hotels located above two small lakes. From the first hotel, the trail leads uphill onto the Piani del Rosett and then reaches Lago Rosset (Lake Rosset). This is the largest and most easily found lake of the many on the plateau; the others, with the exception of Lago Nero, which is in another valley to the north, are not too hard to find with the contour map. You will have higher views and reach more lakes by following the trail up towards the Col del Leynir.

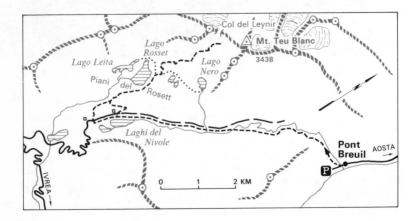

Li Trebecchi (lakes). The top of Gran Paradiso is lost in clouds

*A stone beside the trail,
carved in 1885*

86 MONTE BIANCO VIEW

**One way to Courmayeur 13 km, 8 miles
Hiking time 4½ hours
High point 2375 meters, 7790 feet
Elevation gain 600 meters, 1986 feet
Map D&R Massif du Mont Blanc 2**

Walk along the side of a high ridge and absorb breathtaking views of the south face of Mont Blanc or, as the Italians call it, Monte Bianco. This exciting trail is part of the Tour Du Mont Blanc (Hike No. 18). Of course, you can have much the same view by riding any of the three cable cars which leave from the towns of Entreves and Courmayeur; but the slow pace of foot travel allows you to participate in the evolving views. Thanks to local bus service, you can make this a one-way hike from Val Veni to Courmayeur; or you can hike up a seldom used trail to the top of Mont Fortin, a 2758-meter-high mountain.

At Courmayeur take the Val Veni bus for 11 km to the end of the pavement. The trailhead is just across the stone bridge, elevation 1955 meters. Even from there the views are superb; and they get better as the well defined trail swings upward. In 1 km cross a stream on a foot log; at 1½ km you reach an abandoned farm and an unmarked junction. A look at the map is helpful at this point. One trail goes to Mont Fortin, a good alternate hike; by facing west you can see this rarely used trail switchbacking up broad slopes into a narrow gully to the summit. The main trail continues up from the farmhouse to a 2375-meter-high shoulder of Mont Favre, about 2½ km from the trailhead. By this time the views have unfolded The Mont Blanc de Courmayeur looms across the valley and so do at least five huge glaciers that spill off this massive cone. To the northeast in

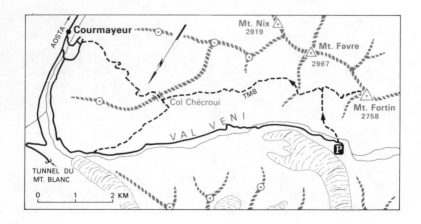

Bianco massif

the Val Ferret (see Hike No. 87) the Grandes Jorasses dominate the scene. All along the route other views compete for your attention. At about 7½ km from the start, the trail drops down to the 1956-meter-high Col Checroui. Here there is a choice of two trails, each pleasant. The left one descends 3 km through woods to a bus stop on the Val Veni road; the right fork descends for 5½ km to Courmayeur itself.

87 GRAND COL FERRET

Round trip 9 km, 5½ miles
Hiking time 5 hours
High point 2537 meters, 8321 feet
Elevation gain 774 meters, 2539 feet
Map D&R Massif du Mont Blanc and Beaufortain; Courmayeur 292

Located below some of the highest and most dramatic peaks in the Alps, this hike starts in a forest of larch trees and climbs through spacious green meadows to a high pass on the Italian-Swiss border. It's one section of the week-long tour around Mont Blanc (Hike No. 18). In season, the green meadows are speckled with wildflowers—yellow buttercups, rose-colored louseworts, tiny blue forget-me-nots, asters, moss campion—to mention only a few of the many species.

From Courmayeur drive up the main highway past the village of Entreves, and at the last switchback before the Mont Blanc tunnel turn right into the Val Ferret. A town bus runs up the Val Ferret as far as Lavachey. If you have a car you can drive up as far as Arnuva to a parking space, elevation 1770 meters. The road is spectacular, even though this once completely wild valley is slowly becoming filled with campgrounds, playground swings for children, and cappuccino parlors. The partly forested and flowered meadows of the valley floor are overwhelmed by one of the longest, highest walls in Europe, the southern flanks of the Mont Blanc massif, punctuated by the needles of rock rising above the Glacier de la Brenva. Those walking the road will find much to stare at. The road ends and the rocky trail, well defined and marked here and there with the red and white paint stripes that signal the Tour du Mont Blanc, switchbacks up into steep meadows. The views of glaciers and peaks—the Grandes Jorasses, the Aiguille du Geant, and the Peuterey Ridge—change with the altitude gain. The hiker reaches the cairn marking the Italian-Swiss border at the Grand Col Ferret, 2537 meters, 4½ km from the parking area. From the pass there are splendid views of French, Italian, and Swiss peaks, including the imposing Grand Combin. The trail continuing the Tour Du Mont Blanc winds down into the Swiss Val Ferret; if you choose to go there, you can make your way back to Italy by foot, bus, or train from there. Otherwise, retrace your steps down the Italian side.

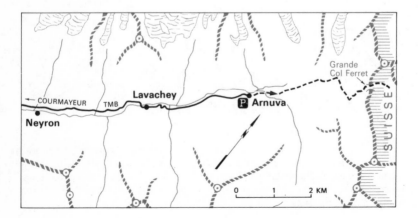

Hikers near the Grand Col Ferret

88 MONTE CERVINO

Round trip 12 km, 7½ miles
Hiking time 4 hours
High point 2516 meters, 8252 feet
Elevation gain 1500 meters, 4920 feet
Map IGC Torino 5 Cervino Monte Rosa
   Kompass Carta 87 Breuil-Cervinia-Zermatt

On this hike you walk through flower-covered meadows overlooking the towering peak of Monte Cervino, the Italian name for the Matterhorn. That dramatic peak, shared by Switzerland and Italy and so full of mountain lore, is surrounded by an inspiring ring of glaciers, including those on the Dent d'Herens to the west and the long ice-covered ridge to the east punctuated by the Theodul Pass. Since the Italian town of Cervinia is a ski and summer resort, there are cable cars to take you up through beautiful country. However, you will more fully appreciate these wonderful views by walking and climbing.

Fortunately, the best hike in the area is not disturbed by the scars of mechanical transport. Leave the Torino-Aosta expressway at the town of Chatillon and take the road marked "Cervinia" to the large parking lot on the outskirts of Cervinia, elevation 2000 meters. From there, walk toward the main part of town to a junction near the church. Go uphill about 100 meters; switchback left, then right past the entrance to the cable car station. At this point there are two ancient trail signs which read "Colle Sre Cime Bianche," and "Plan Maison-Lago Goillet." Head left past the Petit Palais Hotel and follow a rough service road that deteriorates with each meter of vertical gain. At about 3 km the "road" reaches some farm buildings situated on a green knoll overlooking the town. In July, this knoll is covered with lovely wildflowers: anemones, violas, gentians, buttercups, and a few clumps of moss campion here and there. Continue to follow the ruts of the abandoned road. Eventually, the trail crosses a narrow-gauge railroad which was probably used to bring equipment for constructing the reservoir. At about 5 km you reach Lago Goillet, the reservoir, elevation 2516 meters. Walk around the far end of the lake for the stunning view of Monte Cervino reflected in the water.

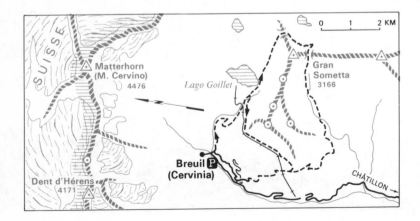

The Matterhorn and flower field

From here you can climb to the rocky summit of the hill above, or return to town. To get to town, follow the railroad tracks, which contour westward around the hillside, and then take the trail back to Cervinia. You will reach the Pista di Bob (bobsled track), and from there it's a short walk up the highway to the starting point.

From the reservoir there is also a longer loop passing several small lakes; but when we were there in July the trail was buried in snow. So we just spent the final hours of the day enjoying the flowers, reflections, and the views.

89 SENTIERO ROMA

Round trip 36 km, 22½ miles
Hiking time 3 days
High point 2765 meters, 9069 feet
Elevation gain 5400 meters, 17,712 feet (cumulative)

Rifugio Ponti round trip 7 hours
Rifugio Allevi round trip 8 hours
Map Kompass Carta 92 Chiavenna-Val Bregaglia and 93 Bernina-Sondrio

On the sunny side of the Bregaglia Alps, a rugged trail, the Sentiero Roma, goes around the head of the Val Masino under granite peaks that straddle the Swiss-Italian border. The cliffs are massive, the pinnacles sharp, and the glaciers relatively small.

This poorly marked trail is difficult—only very experienced hikers should try it. It's a high trail, crossing boulder fields and hard patches of snow. The seven passes to cross vary from easy to difficult. However, when the way gets very bad, there are strategically placed steel cables for handholds and iron spikes for footholds. And there are alternate trails heading down to the valley.

The complete loop trip takes 3 full days. Three refuges along the way serve meals and offer shelter, and there are also two unattended huts. You can walk the trip in either direction, but since there is bus service to Bagni del Masino, the highest point reached by road, this is the logical starting point. To get there, turn off highway 38 between Sondrio and Lago di Como at the small town of Masino. Follow signs to the Val Masino and San Martino.

If you just want to sample this rugged area, you can select a 1- or 2-day hike. Try either the 4½-hour climb (the sign says 3½ hours) to the Rifugio C. Ponti, or the 5-hour trek to the Rifugio Allevi. Both start in farmyards and work their way through forest to meadows and onto barren rock and snow.

If you have a car, drive to the Rifugio Ponti trail, which for the time being starts at elevation 1200 meters, at a point where the road is blocked by a massive rockslide. Until the slide is cleared away, getting to the rifugio involves a 10-km climb up 1400 vertical

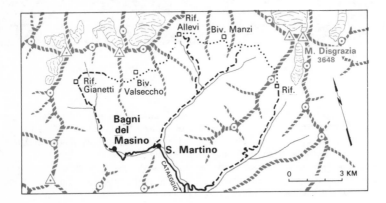

Fog-covered peaks near Rifugio Allevi

meters. The Rifugio Allevi is reached from San Martino, elevation 923 meters, by a dirt road going up the Valle di Mello. The road is so rough it is best not to drive it; but you will have time to enjoy a lovely river as it cascades over rocks and swells occasionally into deep, clear pools. The road turns into a trail, crosses several farm yards, and at 4 km leaves the valley floor. Now it climbs seriously with switchbacks to the refuge at 2385 meters, approximately 10 km, an elevation gain of 1460 meters.

Even if you do not wish to walk the entire Sentiero Roma, spending a night at one of the huts will give you a chance to explore this route and hike at least a section of it.

90 HINTER-SCHONECK
Stelvio National Park

Round trip 14 km, 9 miles
Hiking time 6 hours
High point 3128 meters, 10,260 feet
Elevation gain 1300 meters, 4264 feet
Map Kompass Wanderkarte 52

Climb to the summit of Hinter-Schoneck, a 3128-meter-high mountain, to a breathtaking panorama of glaciers, mountains, and valleys in Stelvio National Park. While most trails in the area are heavily hiked and climbed, this one is not.

By Post Bus or auto, travel to the small village of Gomago on highway 38, between the village of Spondinig and the Stilfser Joch (pass). At Gomago turn onto a paved road signed "Solda/Sulden" and go to the village of St. Gertraud. Parking space at the

Konig-Spitz and Suldenferner (Glacier) from Stieralm

trailhead is extremely limited, so it may be best to park near the bus stop close to the large church. Then walk east across the Suldenbach River on the highway bridge and head uphill to the trailhead near the Hotel Post Zum Ortler, at approximately 1850 meters' elevation.

Directly across the highway from the hotel take trail 6 uphill, toward Hotel Merlet. Just beyond this second hotel turn left onto trail 19, going toward Marcia/Marasch, a big wide path which climbs steeply through forest. About 2 km from the trailhead, trail 19 joins trail 18. Soon after, the forest thins and you pass the timberline at 2½ km, elevation 2248 meters, at the Stieralm. From there, the wide trail contours north around the hillside. Just beyond the first farm building, locate an obscure trail climbing up, marked with yellow stripes painted on rocks. Many of the rocks are set on end, and in places where the trail disappears only the yellow marks indicate the way. The farther one goes, the more definite the trail becomes as it climbs a shoulder of Vorder Schoneck. Near the top of this 2908-meter peak, the trail contours up toward up Hinter Schoneck. If you are short of time, walk to the summit of the lower peak, where you will have a fairly good view. Of course, it will be better from the higher peak; so if you have time, continue on the trail through rubble and flower fields to the 3128-meter-high summit, approximately 7 km from the trailhead. Although there are still higher points on the ridge, this is high enough. The views from the summit are superb. To the east and south are peaks with glaciers, some of them very large; but the most unusual is the Ortler to the west, a 3905-meter peak of rock, snow, and glaciers. On the north ridge you can see the Rifugio G. Payer.

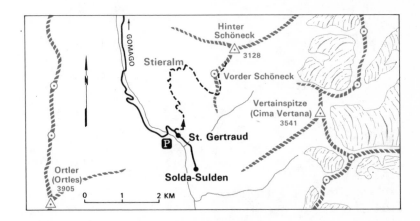

91 RIFUGIO G. PAYER
Stelvio National Park

One way 10½ km, 6½ miles
Hiking time 6 hours
High point 3020 meters, 9906 feet
Elevation gain 1170 meters, 3838 feet
Map Kompass Wanderkarte 52

Rifugio G. Payer on left. Ortler (Mountain), right

The Ortler Gruppe are high glacier-covered peaks in Stelvio National Park near the Swiss-Italian border. The highest peak is the 3905-meter Ortler. Below its summit is the Rifugio G. Payer, perched on a razor-sharp ridge at 3020 meters, a popular hut for hikers and climbers alike. Views from there are sensational.

Bus and auto directions are the same as those for Hinter-Schoneck (Hike No. 90). In the town of St. Gertraud, find the Pension Bambi and a parking lot just below the church, elevation 1850 meters. The trailhead can be found at a dirt road at the upper end of the parking lot. Take trail 4, which at first is also trail 8.

The trail soon splits. Go uphill on trail 4 which, after ½ km, passes a junction with trail 21 and at 1½ km passes a junction with trail 13. Continue uphill through thinning forest; the trail soon enters open meadow with a large talus slope to the right and Mount Ortler towering straight above. Up to the right you will see the Tabaretta Hutte. After passing several more junctions, the trail leaves the open talus slope and switchbacks up the final grass slope to the Tabaretta Hutte, elevation 2536 meters, 4 km from the parking lot. The way from there up to the Rifugio G. Payer is narrow and often steep, with several slide areas. The trail crosses a high pass at 2877 meters. You can see across the valley many of the 48 switchbacks leading to Stelvio Pass. At 5½ km you arrive at the 3020-meter-high Rifugio G. Payer.

If transportation is not a problem, descend to Trafoi, a small village on the road to the Stelvio Pass; it is well known as the birthplace of the famous Italian skier Gustavo Thoeni. The trail to Trafoi is unmarked. It takes off below the final ascent to the Rifugio G. Payer, switchbacking down through boulders and talus. At ½ km there is a poorly marked intersection with a trail to the left leading to the Bergl Hutte or Rifugio A. Borletti. (This trail, number 18, crosses several large snowfields, and should not be followed until you have asked and found out about its condition.)

The other route down, the main trail, continues to the right past the service lift (for the Payer hut) and an abandoned hut at 1½ km. The trail is kept in good shape for the pack horses that bring goods up to the lift. At 3½ km the trail passes another abandoned hut, noted on the map as an operating guest hut. At 4½ km a confusing area of crisscrossing trails begins; you would do well to head down in as straight a line as possible until you reach the Trafoibach (river). From there climb a short hill to Trafoi, elevation 1543 meters, 5 km from the Payer hut.

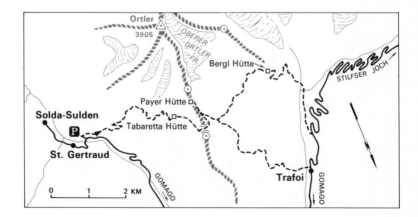

92 DOLOMITI DI BRENTA

Round trip to Rifugio Brentei 12 km, 7½ miles
Hiking time 4½ hours
High point 2120 meters, 6954 feet
Elevation gain 600 meters, 1968 feet
Map Kompass Carta 073 Dolomiti di Brenta

Located on the western end of the Dolomites, the Brenta massif is endowed with a beauty all its own. Perhaps this is because these mountains are altered coral reefs which were pushed up from the sea millions of year ago. Unlike many summits in the Swiss and French Alps, Dolomite summits are often round. The rock is softer and has a reddish-grey color.

In the Brenta massif the hiking is quite varied, with trails to suit all tastes; all have excellent views. Easy day hikes follow wide trails with an occasional tunnel or handrail. On sunny weekends there are thousands of hikers on these trails, from children carried in packsacks to grandmothers wearing long dresses accompanied by teenage girls in bikinis. The difficult trails go along high ledges where there are cable handholds that experienced hikers can manage with relative ease. Often steps have been cut in the rock: steel footholds and handholds—as well as steel ladders, tunnels, and bridges—are common. Exposure can be frightening. A short rope and carabiner are essential; and a hard hat is recommended. If you are excited by these kinds of trails, try them in August when the snow has melted from the steep gullies. Otherwise, stick to the lower trails.

The Brenta Dolomites are reached from the town of Madonna di Campiglio, located on road 239 just off highway 42 between Bozon and the Tonale Pass. To start, try the climb up to the Rifugio Brentie, a good base camp for the more experienced backpacker who wants to set off on 2- to 3-day loop hikes.

At Madonna di Campiglio cross the stream on a city street, head downhill a short way, and follow signs to the road's end at the Rifugio Vallesinella, elevation 1513 meters. There is a choice of two trails, both going to Rifugio Casinei. Trail 317 is only 1½ km long, but is steep and badly eroded; trail 381-376 is almost twice as long, but is in

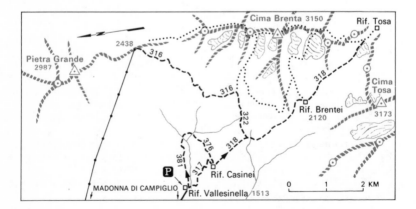

Trail to Rifugio Brentei

excellent condition—its grade is moderate and the hiking time is about the same as for trail 317. Having tried both, we recommend the longer route.

From Rifugio Casinei, follow the wide and well graded trail 318 another 3 km up. It climbs steeply at first, then contours around hillsides, goes along ledges with cable handrails, and passes through a tunnel to the Rifugio Brentei, elevation 2120 meters. The same trail continues another 2 km, then becomes a scramble on rock until it reaches the Rifugio Tosa and various loop trips. A short distance past the Rifugio Brentei, you can pick out above you on the rock wall the Via delle Bocchette trail, which traverses the face of the cliff. This is one medium-level cable route.

For more details of the cable routes, read the Sierra Club's totebook, *Huts and Hikes in the Dolomites* by Ruth Rudner.

93 VAL NAMBINO LAKES LOOP

Loop trip 12 km, 7½ miles
Hiking time 5 hours
High point 2400 meters, 7872 feet
Elevation gain 750 meters, 2460 feet
Map Kompass Carta 073 Dolomiti di Brenta

For a completely different perspective of the Brenta Dolomites, hike into the mountains west of Madonna di Campiglio. From there you can see the entire Brenta Gruppe—magnificent needles and snowcapped peaks. You will also see a striking contrast between the rock you are looking at and the rock where you are standing. Whereas the Brenta Gruppe are dolomite rock with water disappearing into underground channels, in these western mountains the rock is a form of granite. The water runs in numerous streams; thanks to the scooping effect of ancient glaciers, many lakes have formed. The lakes are what distinguish this hike.

The hike starts just outside the town of Madonna di Campiglio (see directions for Hike No. 92). You can gain considerable elevation by taking a cable car from the city, but then you will miss the lovely Lago (lake) di Nambino. So find the road marked Val Nambino at the outskirts of town and drive 1 km to a junction. Take the right-hand fork and park, elevation 1650 meters. Walk the road to its end, then climb a badly eroded trail to Lago di Nambino, about 1½ km. This lovely lake is surrounded by forest and meadows and it attracts many tourists.

The trip is far from over. Near the outlet of the lake, keep right. Follow the trail as it climbs away from the lake and then switchbacks, circling high above it and offering views of the water and mountains. So far the going is easy; but eventually the trail steepens, and with a series of short switchbacks it climbs into meadows where the track is sketchy. However, numerous patches of paint on the boulders show the way. At about 5 km you reach a knoll overlooking Lago Serodoli di Sopra, elevation 2370 meters. A few meters farther are Lago Gelato and several small ponds. You can take a side trip to Lago del Nambrone, farther up the valley. But to continue the loop, cross the outlet of Lago Serodoli di Sopra and follow a trail that contours south—and up and down—to

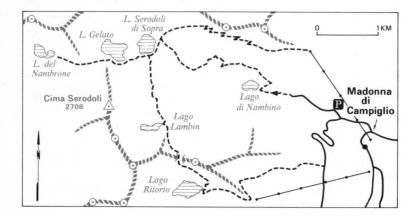

Lago di Nambino. Brenta Dolomites in distance

Lago Lambin. From there continue south over a low pass and drop down to Lago Ritorto at 8 km, elevation 2053 meters. The follow a broad path to the top of a chair lift, where you will find a trail that takes you down to the road and the starting point.

Bridge on climbers' trail to Rifugio Pisciadu

94 SELLA DOLOMITES

One way 7 km, 4¼ miles
Hiking time 3 hours
High point 2260 meters, 7413 feet
Elevation gain 100 meters, 328 feet
Elevation loss 700 meters, 2296 feet
Map Kompass Wanderkarte 59

The best way to explore the Sella Gruppe of the Dolomites is to go by lift from the Passo Pordoi to the Rifugio Maria, and from there, follow trails 627 and 666 past numerous other refuges to the Rifugio Pisciadu, located on top of gigantic cliffs at the range's northern edge. However, to sample the Sella Gruppe, we chose a downhill route at the foot of the northern cliffs which gave us closeup views of two climbing routes up the cliffs and a waterfall. Since this is a one-way hike, it is best to take a bus from the city of Corvara to Passo Gardena, elevation 2137 meters.

At the top of Passo Gardena find the trail on the south side signed "Rifugio Pisciadu." After climbing the grassy knoll approximately 100 meters, the trail starts a gradual descent towards Corvara. In approximately 1 km, there is a junction: on the uphill trail, you climb a steep rocky gully to the Rifugio Pisciadu, crossing snow slopes and climbing a cliff with the aid of iron steps, cables, and carabiners. Although this trail is used by hundreds of hikers every day, it crosses a potentially dangerous snow slope; we recommend staying on the lower trail.

Continue downhill on the lower trail and cross the gully. The way is poorly marked. Don't be confused by a trail coming up from the valley floor, or by a well used trail heading for the waterfall. The route to Corvara continues down on an unmarked and rather obscure trail. (Before going farther, you might walk over to the waterfall for a look at the trail which climbs to the Rifugio Pisciadu. You will see that a few climbers wear hard hats and hook onto the cables with carabiners; unfortunately, most people who use this route are not that cautious.) The down trail crosses

Trail near Passo Gardena

under the falls and in 3 km from the pass reaches a junction. The trail switchbacks down a very steep gully to a wide path near the Rio Pisciadu (river) and then through forest and meadows to the city of Corvara.

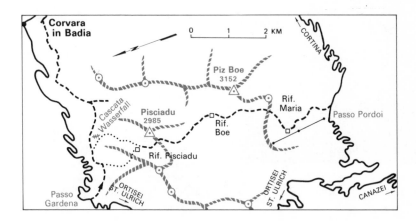

95 PUEZ DOLOMITES

One way 11 km, 7 miles
Hiking time 5 hours
High point 2528 meters, 8294 feet
Elevation gain 390 meters, 1279 feet
Elevation loss 954 meters, 3130 feet
Map Kompass Wanderkarte 59

Hikers on the cable route

Compared to the many breathtaking areas in the Dolomites, the Puez Gruppe might be considered of secondary interest, but that is not necessarily the case. Once you are past the border peaks, you enter a broad plateau, with meadows frequently interrupted by white limestone outcroppings formed as either horizontal weathered sheets or low-lying vertical ribs. Close inspection of the stone shows that it is full of fossils. There are several small lakes, high rounded hills, rock caps, and a deep canyon-like valley called the Vallelunga which cuts the plateau. Many well marked trails provide ample sport for the ambitious, adventurous wanderer. And several small huts offer sleeping space for early arrivals. So this plateau is not without interest.

From the city of Corvara, take the bus to Passo Gardena, elevation 2137 meters. The trailhead is opposite the Rifugio Alpino. Head north on trail 2, marked "Rifugio Puez." This begins as a dirt road going up to the Rifugio Cir and a chair lift. Walk along the road for a short distance; after a switchback, follow a trail to the right across green pastureland. At ½ km the trail forks bewilderingly: two branches of trail 2 take off. Either way is all right. On the left fork, you climb past the cross on the skyline with the aid of cables.

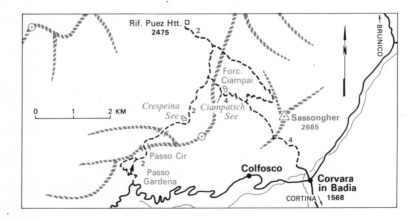

Passo Gardena and the Sella Dolomites from trail on Puez Dolomites

The right fork is easier, and at 1 km the trail winds around a small basin filled with fantastic rock pillars. A quick side trip to the left is worth the extra time because of the excellent views it offers. The trail arrives at the Passo Cir, elevation 2466 meters, where you can see the snowcapped Sella Gruppe. A bit farther on at the 2528-meter-high Passo Crespeina, there are good views of the plateau-like midsection of the Puez Gruppe. Below the pass is Lago Crespeina; beyond the lake, the trail crosses a rolling landscape until it reaches a pass, Forcella Ciampai, elevation 2388 meters, at 4½ km. The pass lies at the head of two deep valleys. Trail 4, which is the best and easiest route back to Corvara, starts here. On the way the trail passes a small lake called the Ciampatsch See and ends on a paved road in a group of houses above the city.

If you choose to continue to the Rifugio Puez, stay on trail 2, crossing the pass. After walking 6½ km, you arrive at the hut which in itself is unimpressive; however, it is a useful place to stay, and you can branch out from it onto numerous trails.

96 SEXTENER DOLOMITES

One way 13 km, 8 miles
Hiking time 8 hours
High point 2622 meters, 8603 feet
Elevation gain (estimated) 800 meters, 2625 feet
Map Kompass Wanderkarte 58

For excitement this hike rivals a roller coaster. It is not for everyone and should be avoided by all but the surefooted. The trail seems to seek out the most hair-raising routes. It leads the hiker to views of deep gorges, down sheer faces of cliff walls to the valley below. It follows shelves along the rocky cliffs; and where there is no natural passage, the trail has been hacked out of the wall itself, often with only 1½ meters (4 or 5 feet) of head room, with metal or wood walkways. The more difficult areas are strung with metal cables that start too late and end too soon. Cliff ascents and descents are aided by ladders. At one point, apparently quite unnecessarily, the trail goes through a tunnel that probably was built as a fortification during World War I.

The excitement of the trail is surpassed only by the views it offers of the impressive stone towers and jagged peaks so characteristic of the Dolomites. Unfortunately, the entire high traverse from Auronzohutte to the Col de Varda should not be attempted until late August or September except by very experienced hikers with mountaineering training. Earlier in the season, hikers should plan to stop halfway at the Rifugio Fratelli Fonda-Savio and then either retrace their steps or take trail 115 to Lago di Misurina (Lake Misurina).

From Lake Misurina (Hike No. 97), elevation 1756 meters, take a bus or drive road 117 to the Auronzohutte parking lot at 2320 meters' elevation. Just below the hut take trail 117 headed south, and signed "Rifugio Fratelli Fonda-Savio." After 1 km it leaves the green meadows, traverses the cliffs, climbs up, down, and across breathtakingly exposed places until at 2½ km it comes to a junction with trail 119 at a small pass, elevation 2206 meters. The trail then heads across a large boulder field up the valley and may cross several small but level snowfields. It forks again, this time with trail 116.

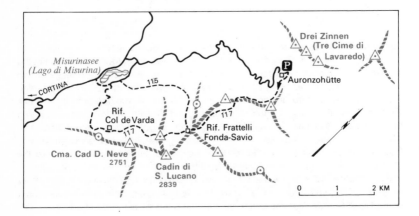

Sextener Dolomites

Keep slightly to the right as you walk toward the cliffs. The trail now splits into three possible routes; the left, marked with blue dots, is the easiest and most logical way. Eventually all three routes rejoin and, the last scramble over, you arrive at the Rifugio Fratelli Fonda-Savio, elevation 2367 meters, 5 km from the start.

Because of the snow, the early season hiker may have to go downhill on the well graded trail in front of the hut; but the late season hiker must ask the hutkeeper or other backpackers if the snow has melted from the slope leading up the first pass, the Forcella del Diavolo, 2622 meters high. If the way is clear, continue on trail 115-117; since the trail goes over loose gravel and rubble, plant each step firmly and with care. After the pass, the trail drops steeply into a narrow valley and intersects the poorly marked trail 118. Still on loose ground, the trail climbs through a 2471-meter-high second pass. crosses a large field of giant, oddly shaped rocks, and arrives at the Rifugio Col de Varda, elevation 2100 meters, 10 km from the start.

The hut is located at the top of a ski run and has a chair lift running up to it year-round. To return to Lake Misurina, take the gravel road, and stay right at the intersection to Citta di Capri; or follow faint paths below the lift, reaching the main road at 13 km.

97 TRE CIME

Loop trip 11 km, 7 miles
Hiking time 5½ hours
High point 2522 meters, 8272 feet
Elevation gain 700 meters, 2296 feet
Map Kompass Wanderkarte 58

Chapel near the Rifugio Locatelli

Since the end of World War 1 the Dolomite Mountains, including part of what was the Austrian Tirol, have been annexed to Italy. Because nationalistic feelings are strong, place names on maps are printed in two languages, and the inhabitants speak three: Italian, German, and the local Ladin. This explains why the Rifugio Antonio Locatelli— one of the highlights of this hike—is also called the Drei Zinnen Hutte and Rifugio Tre Cime di Lavaredo. Whatever language you see or hear, the Dolomites provide some of the best hiking and friendliest atmosphere in the Alps. The mixture of jovial Tiroleans with exuberant Italians accounts for the atmosphere: noisy trails and huts with much laughter and good-natured fun. The Dolomites' scenery adds to the pleasure—beautiful limestone towers and fantastic colors.

The Rifugio Locatelli can be reached from the north or south. From the north, bus service is available to Sesto/Sexten. From there you must catch a taxi up the Fiscalina Valley to the trailhead, and then climb for 6 km to the Locatelli Hut. We traveled by car from the south on the road from Cortina to Dobbiaco, then on road "48 bis" past Lake

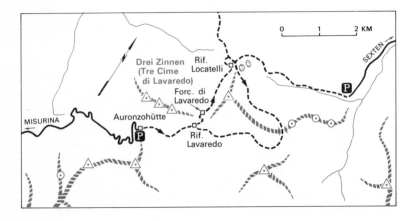

Rifugio Locatelli

Misurina onto route 117. Our destination was the parking area at the Auronzohutte, elevation 2320 meters. If you take this route, after parking your car walk on the service road, trail 161, slightly downhill, under the towering walls of theTre Cime, for 2 km to the Rifugio Lavaredo, elevation 2390 meters. From the hut take trail 101, climbing over the Forcella di Lavaredo (Paternsatel), and then drop down to the Rifugio Locatelli at 2438 meters, 3½ km. The four-storied hut stares out at the spires of Monte Paterno and the three summits.

This hut is an excellent base for several days of excursions. If possible, however, avoid the hut during August when it is overcrowded with hikers and climbers from all over the world.

Of the two main ways back to civilization, we preferred the loop, trail 101. It took us past the two lakes which lie beneath the hut, then climbed the 2522-meter-high Forcella Pran di Cenga. Remnants of the fierce fighting of World War I — caves, old gun emplacements, barbed wire, and rotting buildings — serve as grim memorials in the shadow of majestic mountains.

From there follow trail 104, which leads back to the Rifugio Lavaredo and then down the service road to the parking lot.

Lake Bled from Osojnica trail

98 LAKE BLED

Round trip 3½ km, 2¼ miles
Hiking time 1½ hours
High point 685 meters, 2247 feet
Elevation gain 260 meters, 853 feet
Map Julian Alps, Eastern Part, or the free tourist map

The Alps of northern Yugoslavia are not high compared to the rest of the Alps, but they rise abruptly from valley floors and have a special age-old beauty. This can be discovered through well defined trails, a system of huts called doms, and the friendly mountain people. Unfortunately, the maps, which are readily available from nearby tourist offices, give no indication of trail difficulty. As we found out, some trails turn into cable routes requiring mountaineering skills.

Probably the most photogenic spot in mountainous Yugoslavia is the glacial Blejsko Jezero (Lake Bled) with its small island containing a baroque church. With a rich, thousand-year-old history, the lake and city of Bled have recently become favorite retreats for heads of state and hordes of tourists. The popularity of Lake Bled has not destroyed its subtle beauty.

The resort city of Bled, in the heart of the Julian Alps of northwest Yugoslavia, is reached by road or train. The best view of the lake is from a high hill located at the city's southwest end, near the campground. This is more of a pleasant walk than a hike. There is no bus service around the lake and no parking at the trailhead. Walk from the city or drive out and park near the campground. From there walk south 500 meters to a well graded trail marked "Osojnica 6," elevation 495 meters. The trail winds steeply up through forest to the foot of a bare cliff, which you scale by using an iron stairway with 88 steps. At the top you will have two superb viewpoints for seeing this emerald lake.

After enjoying the views, you may want to continue through the forest another kilometer to the top of Mount Osojnica, a 756-meter-high hill. Unfortunately, the view from the summit is limited, but in mid-July there were many wild cyclamen blooming on the forest floor.

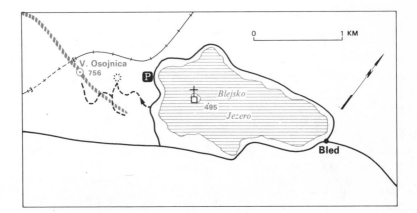

99 MOUNT TRIGLAV (DOM STANICA)
Mount Triglav National Park

Round trip 20 km, 12½ miles
Hiking time 2 days
High point 2332 meters, 7649 feet
Elevation gain 1420 meters, 4658 feet
Map Julian Alps, Eastern part

This hike runs along the flanks of the highest peak in Yugoslavia, Mount Triglav, elevation 2863 meters. Plan to spend several days in the region since there are huts surrounded by a great network of trails. Be especially careful, however: some trails traverse or climb sheer cliffs and these dangers are not indicated on the maps. It's also a good idea to carry water with you.

A good destination for the first day's hike is Dom (hut) Stanica. There are two well marked trails leading to the hut. The trail from the Aljazev Dom is very steep, but it was passable with the aid of an occasional iron spike hold and a cable handrail to negotiate a hair-raising ledge. However, after climbing 800 meters, the trail ended at the bottom of a 100-meter cliff with a steel cable hanging down it. Since this was definitely not for us, we turned back. For our second assault, we went up the Krma Valley. This turned out to be an excellent trail; however, shortly before we reached Dom Stanica, the mountains became engulfed in fog.

Go to the town of Mojstrana between the Italian border and Jesenice. Near the Triglav Hotel, find a dirt road marked "Bled 22, Krma 9." If you are walking, follow the red signs to the Kovinarska Koca (a hotel). If driving, follow the most traveled road to Krma. At 9 km, you pass the hotel and reach the road's end at about 12½ km (slightly shorter if walking), elevation 910 meters.

The trail, used by pack horses to supply the various huts, goes up the valley; it is marked with a red circle and a white dot. It gradually steepens and climbs through forest to a junction. Keep right, climb into rocky meadows to several forest huts and two more junctions. Keep right again, staying on the horse trail. At 2017 meters, 7 km from where

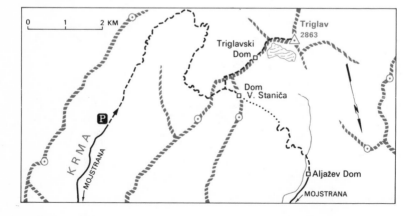

Krma Valley. Tosc (Mountain) in center

the road ended, the terrain changes: vegetation becomes sparse and the rocks are strangely eroded. The grade lessens as the trail rises to a pass at about 2250 meters, 9 km. A bit farther, there is another junction. The left trail follows a ridge to Triglavski Dom and continues up to the summit of Mount Triglav. Take the right trail and continue to Dom Stanica at 2332 meters, almost 10 km from the road's end. Although the hiking time to the dom is only about 5 hours, most people are ready to call it a day.

Because of the fog, our only views of Mount Triglav were on post cards and in books. They looked impressive. The region is fascinating, and the mountain people are very friendly, so it is worth exploring the high trails around Mount Triglav.

100 LEPA KOMNA

Round trip to Krnsko Jezero (lake) 8 km, 5 miles
Hiking time 3½ hours
High point 1463 meters, 4799 feet
Elevation gain 800 meters, 2624 feet

Round trip to Dom Planina na Krau 21 km, 13 miles
Hiking time 2 days
High point 1803 meters, 5914 feet
Elevation gain 1500 meters, 4920 feet
Maps Julian Alps East and West

Krnsko Jezero

The Lepa Komna, in the northwest corner of Yugoslavia, provides a great contrast to the rugged peaks that surround Mount Triglav. This is ideal country for roaming through rich meadows that lie beneath low rounded summits. The whole area is crisscrossed by wagon roads built during World War I and long since overgrown. Still discernible, they pass abandoned barracks, old barbed wire fences, and other relics of tragic periods in history. Water is scarce.

From Kranjski Gora, travel south over Vrsic Pass toward Bovec and find a dirt road heading east, 1¾ km downstream from Soca. It is marked "Lepena 6 km." At the road's end you will find a mountain hut, Dom dr. Klementa Juga, elevation 680 meters. From there the trail is marked "Krn 2245 meters, 4½ hours, Krn Jez 1383 meters, 2 hours, Komna 1525 meters 4½ hours." Partly on wide military wagon roads, the trail climbs steeply, rising 800 meters in an estimated 2 km. At 3½ km you pass a farm and reach a trail junction. Regardless of your final destination, take the right-hand trail another ½ km to Krnsko Jezero, a lovely lake without an outlet, elevation 1383 meters, 4 km from the road. For day hikers, this is a good turnaround point.

To reach Dom Planina na Krau, return to the junction and turn east, climbing first to a pass then across a large green meadow. At 5 km you reach the roofless remnants of a huge barracks and many other small buildings. From there, with more ups than downs, the trail climbs to a 1803-meter-high pass, 7 km from the start. Shortly before the pass, two chamois leaped across the trail in front of us.

From the pass, the trail drops 300 meters in 3½ km to the Dom Planina na Krau, located at the edge of a forest at 1513 meters, 10½ km from the road. You can spend several days here, taking loop trips into Triglavski National Park and hiking up some of the nearby peaks.

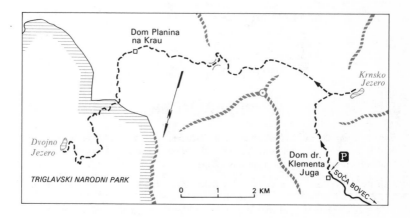

NAMES AND ADDRESSES OF ALPINE CLUBS
(Main branches)

France:	Club Alpin Francais
	9, rue de la Boetie, 75008 Paris
Switzerland:	Geschaftsstelle SAC,
	Helvetiaplatz 4, 3005 Bern
Liechtenstein:	Liechtensteiner Alpenverein,
	F1-9490 Vaduz
Germany:	Deutscher Alpenverein
	Praterinsel 5, 8 Munich 22
Austria:	Osterreichischer Alpenverein,
	Wilhelm-Greil-Strasse 15, 6010 Innsbruck
	(There is also an office in Vienna)
Italy:	Club Alpine Italiano,
	Via Ugo Foscole 3, 20121 Milano
Yugoslavia:	Planinarski Savez Jugoslavija,
	Dobrinjska 10-1, Belgrade

NAMES AND ADDRESSES OF
TRAIL-MANAGING ORGANIZATIONS

GR 10:	Comite National des Sentiers des Grandes Randonnees
	92, rue de Clignancourt
	75883 Paris, FRANCE
GR 5:	CIMES
	14, rue de la Republique
	38027 Grenoble-Cedex, FRANCE

REFERENCES

Evans, Craig: *On Foot Through Europe*. Backpacker, Inc., Bedford Hills, NY, 1979.
This is a "how-to" book with detailed information on transportation, maps, and other important information for hikers.

Reifsnyder, William: *Foot-loose in the Swiss Alps*, Sierra Club, San Francisco, CA, 1974.
This book provides detailed information about many sections of the high traverse from Chamonix, France to Zermatt, Switzerland (Hike No. 24 in this book).

Rudner, Ruth: *Huts and Hikes in the Dolomites*, Sierra Club, San Francisco, CA, 1974.
Here are descriptions of cable routes and other hiking in the Dolomites.